Walter Robson

Rome
the
Empire

Oxford University Press

Oxford University Press, Walton Street, Oxford OX2 6DP

Oxford New York Athens Auckland Bangkok Bombay Calcutta
Cape Town Dar es Salaam Delhi Florence Hong Kong Istanbul
Karachi Kuala Lumpur Madras Madrid Melbourne Mexico City
Nairobi Paris Singapore Taipei Tokyo Toronto

and associated companies in
Berlin Ibadan

Oxford is a trade mark of Oxford University Press

First published 1992
Reprinted 1992, 1995

ISBN 0 19 833546 6

Typeset by MS Filmsetting Limited, Frome, Somerset
Printed in Hong Kong

Acknowledgements

Page 6 Werner Forman Archive; p8 Ancient Art & Architecture
Collection; p9t Bridgeman/Somerset County Museum; p9br & p11bl
AAAC; p11tr Zefa; p12 AAAC; p14bl Michael Holford, br Cambridge
University Collection of Air Photographs; p16r Society of Antiquaries of
London; p18tl Michael Holford; p19tr AAAC, tl Cambridge University
Collection of Air Photographs; p21 & p22bl Werner Forman Archive;
p22tr & cr Michael Holford; p24bl, tr & p26bl AAAC; p26br Mansell
Collection; p27tr AAAC; p28 Michael Holford; p30 Vindolanda Trust;
p31 Mansell Collection; p33c & b Robert Harding Picture Library; p34
C M Dixon; p37 E T Archive; p38 & p39 Werner Forman Archive; p40
Cambridge University Collection of Air Photographs; p41bl & br AAAC;
p42 & p44tl, br Michael Holford; p44cl, bl AAAC; p46tl National
Museum of Wales, bl Michael Holford, br Mansell Collection; p48tl
Michael Holford, b Scala; p49tr Museum of Antiquaries, Newcastle-upon-
Tyne; p51cl, bl AAAC; p52tl Michael Holford, © Rheinisches Landes-
museum, Trier; p53 Mansell Collection; p54 & p55cr AAAC; p57cl Scala,
cr E T Archive; p58bl Michael Holford; p59 Scala; p60 Bridgeman/
Metropolitan Museum, New York; p61t AAAC, bl, br & p62cl Werner
Forman Archive; p63tr E T Archive, bl Michael Holford, cr Colchester &
Essex Museum; p64 & p65 AAAC; p66 Werner Forman Archive; p67tr
E T Archive, b AAAC; p68 Bridgeman/British Museum; p69 Werner
Forman Archive; p70t Michael Holford, b Scala; p71 British Museum; p72
Rheinisches Landesmuseum, Trier; p73 Bridgeman; p74 Robert Harding
Picture Library; p75bl, br Michael Holford; p76t Zefa, b Robert Harding
Picture Library; p77 AAAC; p79bl Michael Holford, br Bridgeman/
Galleria degli Uffizi, Florence.

Front cover: *Death of Caesar* (1859) by Jean-Léon Gérôme. Walters Art
Gallery, Baltimore.

Abbreviation: AAAC = Ancient Art & Architecture Collection.

The illustrations are by Peter Kent and Duncan Storr

Contents

Preface

The title of this series is *Access to History*, and accessibility is its keynote — accessibility to National Curriculum History, in terms of both the Programme of Study and the Attainment Target.

The exercises, which refer to the text, sources, and illustrations, are intended to extend factual knowledge, promote comprehension, and develop a range of skills, all consistent with the National Curriculum Key Elements. The 'criteria grid' (at the end of the book) shows how the individual exercises relate to the Key Elements.

It is not expected that pupils will work through the book unaided. Teachers will wish to omit some exercises and amend others. They will probably decide that some exercises which are set for individual work would be tackled more successfully by using a group or class approach, with the teacher him/herself as leader. The book's aim is to provide teachers with a useful set of resources, not to usurp their role.

The exercises with the fill-in blanks may be either photocopied to provide answer sheets and homework assignments, or copied out by the pupils and filled in as they go along.

1 Fact and Fiction

A AD and BC

We count time from the birth of Jesus Christ. We say that he was born in the year AD 1. The letters 'AD' stand for 'Anno Domini', which is Latin for 'in the year of Our Lord'. No-one in the time of Jesus talked about AD, or counted the years that way. But we now say that nearly 2,000 years have passed since Jesus was born.

We say that the year before AD 1 was 1 BC. The letters 'BC' stand for 'Before Christ', and we count backwards from 1 BC. The year 55 BC was 55 years before the birth of Jesus, and the year 200 BC was 200 years before Jesus.

Now try Exercise 1.1.

Exercise 1.1

Read **Section A.** Write out these dates and events in the right order (earliest first) in the blank spaces.

Date	Event	Date	Event
509 BC	Legend says that Rome became a republic.	....	
27 BC	Augustus became first Roman emperor.		
241 BC	Rome got control of Sicily		
753 BC	Legend says that Rome was founded by Romulus.		
AD 43	Roman conquest of Britain began.		
AD 313	Romans allowed to be Christians.		
AD 407	Last Roman soldiers left Britain.		
AD 122	Emperor Hadrian visited Britain.		

B Legends

Legends are stories about the past. They are handed down from parents to children, and told over and over again. At first, some of the stories were largely true. But as time passes, details get changed, and new bits are added. After hundreds of years, there is not much truth left.

Here are three legends (Aeneas, Romulus and Remus, and Tarquin the Proud) about early Rome.

Aeneas

After ten years' war, the **Greek** army captured **Troy**. (Look at the Map.) The Greeks killed the Trojan men, made slaves of the women, and burned the city. Only a few Trojans escaped, led by a prince called **Aeneas**. For years, the Trojans sailed to and fro. At last, they landed in **Italy**, where Aeneas founded a new city. This was to be the home of the **Latin** people.

Now read Sources 1a and 1b.

Source 1a

Proud Troy fell and lay smoking in ruins. Those of us who survived had to flee to other lands. We built ships on the shore, not knowing where they would take us. In tears, I left the land where Troy once stood.

From a long poem called *The Aeneid*, written by the Roman poet, Virgil. Virgil lived from 70 BC to 19 BC.

Source 1b

Aeneas will fight a great war in Italy and beat strong enemies. He will found a new city there and build its walls. He will live there for three more years. Then his son Ascanius will reign for thirty years. He will move to a new, stronger city, called Alba Longa.

Also from *The Aeneid*. In this part, the god Jupiter is telling what will happen in the future.

THE MEDITERRANEAN

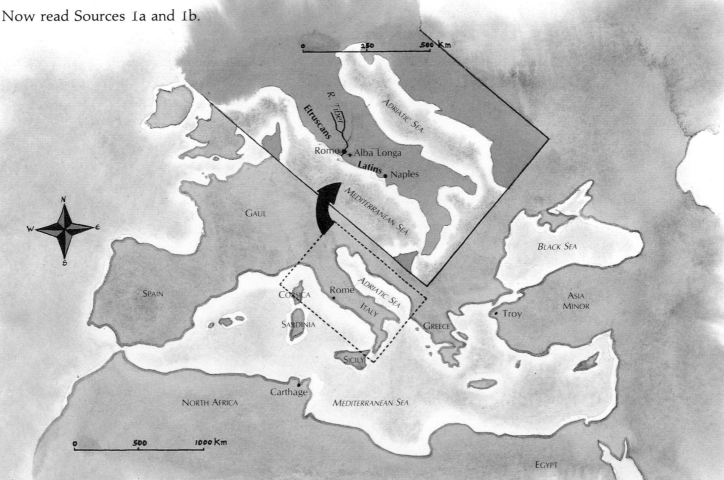

Source 1c

Romulus and Remus with the wolf. The bronze wolf was made by an Etruscan craftsman. Another artist added the twins two thousand years later

Romulus and Remus

Hundreds of years later, **Numitor** was the Latin king of Alba Longa. (Look at the Map on page 5.) He had a daughter, and she had twin sons, called **Romulus** and **Remus**. (Their father was the god Mars.) Numitor also had a brother, and the brother seized the throne. The new king then said that the twins had to be put to death.

Servants put the baby boys in a basket, and left them by the river **Tiber**, where the waters would rise and drown them. But the basket floated, and the twins were carried downstream. They were found on the river bank by a wolf, which fed them. (Look at Source 1c.) Later, they were brought up by a shepherd and his wife.

Romulus and Remus grew up to be strong and brave. They fought for Numitor, and put him back on his throne. Then, in 753 BC, they began to build a new city, on the hills beside the Tiber. But as they were working on the walls, the twins fell out. Remus said that his brother's walls were too low, and jumped over them to prove it. This made Romulus angry, and he killed his brother. Then he finished the city, and became its king. The city's name was **Rome.**

Tarquin the Proud

Rome had seven kings. Romulus was the first, and the last three were **Etruscans**. (Look at the Map on page 5.) The third Etruscan king was **Tarquin**, a high and mighty man whom the Romans hated. They called him **Tarquin the Proud**, and said that he was a **tyrant**. In 509 BC the Romans rebelled. They threw Tarquin out, and Rome became a **republic** (a state with no king).

Now try Exercises 1.2 and 1.3.

Exercise 1.2

Study **the map on page 5**. Read the questions, then write the answers in the blank spaces. (Use words from list below.)

> north   south   east   west   centre   north-east
> north-west   south-east   south-west   Mediterranean
> Italy   Greece   Tiber

a Where is Rome? In the _____ of Italy.

b Which sea would you cross if you sailed from Rome to Spain? _____

c Where is Sicily? To the _____ of Rome.

d Which direction would a ship sailing from Egypt to Rome take? _____ at first, then _____

e Rome lies on which river? _____

f Where did the Etruscans live? To the _____ of Rome.

g Where did the Latins live? To the _____ of Rome.

Exercise 1.3

Read the legends of Aeneas, Romulus, and Tarquin on pages 5 and 7, then answer the questions *in sentences*.

a Which Roman poet told the story of Aeneas?

b Aeneas was supposed to have come from which city?

c Which city is mentioned in Source 1b and in the Romulus story?

d What did the wolf do for Romulus and Remus?

e Why did Romulus kill Remus?

f How many kings of Rome were Etruscans?

g What was the name of Rome's last king?

C The facts

Archaeologists (see **Source 1d**) have dug on the hills beside the Tiber. They have explored the remains of huts and the graves of the people who lived in them. They have found weapons, tools, scraps of pottery, and jewellery. These finds help them to say who the people were, and when they lived there.

These experts tell us that Rome began in about 750 BC. Early Rome was a collection of simple huts. The farmers who lived there had a king, and fought wars with their neighbours. Rome may well have been the leader of a group of Latin cities. There were no city walls at that time. (The name 'Rome' may come from 'Romulus'. Archaeologists have found no trace of Aeneas.)

Between about 600 BC and 500 BC, though, there are signs that the Etruscans took over. The Etruscans were a civilized nation. They could read and write, and knew how to build in stone. They made fine pottery and metal objects. Trade with the Greeks made them rich, and Greek craftsmen lived among them.

Between 600 BC and 500 BC, Rome got its first stone buildings, its first streets, and its first stone temples. A proper **forum** (or market place) was set out. All this building must have been done by Rome's Etruscan kings. But in about 500 BC, the Etruscans lost control. Words carved on a temple in Rome say that the last king was thrown out. Monarchy (rule by kings) came to an end in Rome.

Now try Exercise 1.4.

Source **1d**

Archaeologists at work. Archaeologists search carefully for remains of the past. They dig up parts of buildings, pieces of pottery, coins, weapons and tools. They make a note of what they find and where they find it. Their work can help to show that stories about the past are either true or untrue.

This mosaic pavement is from a Roman Villa in Dorset. It tells the story of Aeneas.

Exercise 1.4

Students of history want to find out the **truth** about the past. **Fiction** (made-up stories) is not the same as history.

Read **Section C**, and think again about what you read in **Section B**. Then note down your answers to these questions.

a Do legends help students of history, or are they just stories?
b What do archaeologists do? How does their work help history? (Look at **Source 1d**.)
c Have archaeologists proved that Aeneas, Romulus, and Remus:
   i were real people?
   ii did not exist?
d In what ways are the legends right about early Rome? How are they wrong?
e What makes the archaeologists think that the Etruscans did control Rome for a time?
f Which parts of the story of Tarquin are true? Which parts may be fiction?

Discuss your answers with others in a group. Then, members of the group could give short talks to the rest of the class, saying what your answers to the questions are, or you could make a group tape.

An Etruscan bronze model of a farmer, his plough, and his two oxen.

Exercise 1.5

Write eight sentences to show that you know what these words mean:

a Legend   **e** Tyrant
b Fact   **f** Republic
c Pottery   **g** Temple
d Inscription   **h** Monarchy

2 The Empire

A From city to empire

At first, Rome was just one of the cities of central Italy. Most of its people were farmers. They kept animals and grew crops in the fields around the city. They were often at war, and they did not always win. In 386 BC, most of Rome was burned by the **Gauls** from the north.

In time Rome's farmers grew into tough soldiers. They were always ready to lay down the plough and pick up the sword. They fought bravely, obeyed orders, and were prepared to die for their city.

The army made Rome the strongest city in Italy. By 270 BC, it controlled all the centre and most of the south. Then there was a clash with **Carthage**. (Look at the Map.) Carthage was a great city in north Africa. Its people were sailors and merchants. They had bases as far away as the east coast of Spain.

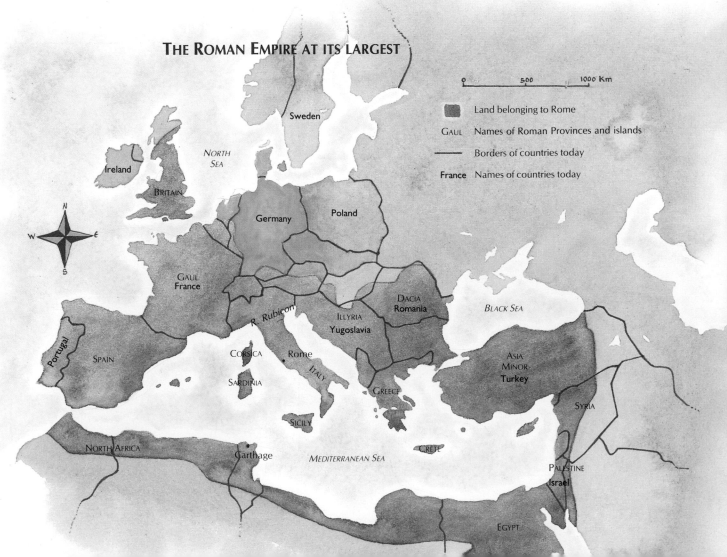

THE ROMAN EMPIRE AT ITS LARGEST

0   500   1000 Km

Land belonging to Rome

GAUL   Names of Roman Provinces and islands

Borders of countries today

France   Names of countries today

Rome and Carthage fought three wars. The hardest for the Romans was the second, just before 200 BC. **Hannibal**, Carthage's greatest general, invaded Italy. He beat the Romans in battle, but he did not have enough men to capture Rome. In the end, it was the Romans who won. By the end of the third war, in 146 BC, Carthage was destroyed. Its empire belonged to Rome.

Now no army could beat Rome's well-armed, well-trained troops. They turned east, and conquered the **civilized** people of Greece, Asia Minor, and Syria. They turned west, and conquered the **barbarians** of central Spain and Gaul. (Look at Source 2a.) All the land round the Mediterranean Sea belonged to Rome.

Now try Exercise 2.1.

Source **2b**

An aqueduct (for transporting water) in Segovia, Spain. It was built in the reign of the Emperor Trajan (AD 96–117).

Source **2a**

This is the tombstone of a Roman cavalryman (horse-soldier). It shows a Roman killing a barbarian. To the Romans, people who did not speak Latin or Greek, and who did not live in towns or cities, were 'barbarians'.

Exercise 2.1

Read **Section A** and study the **Map**. Then answer the questions.

a What was the Roman name for the country we call France? _____

b The Roman province of Illyria was part of which modern country? _____

c Part of what we call Romania belonged to Rome. What did the Romans call it? _____

d Roman 'Asia' was part of the country we call what?

_____

e Name two Roman provinces at the east end of the Mediterranean Sea. _____ and

_____

f Name two large islands in the Mediterranean Sea which belonged to Rome. _____ and

_____

g Name one modern European country which was *not* part of the Roman empire. _____

B The end of the republic

A sculpture of Julius Caesar, made out of bronze.

The republic of Rome was ruled by its **senate**. The senators were the richest men in Rome. Two of them, called **consuls**, had extra power. But the consuls were changed each year. The senators did not want anyone to become too strong.

But some men did. They were the generals who led Rome's armies. **Pompey,** who won wars in Asia Minor and swept the pirates from the sea, became a great hero. So did **Julius Caesar,** who conquered Gaul.

Pompey and Caesar were friends at first. Then they quarrelled. In 49 BC,

Caesar marched his army towards Rome. When he crossed the river **Rubicon**, he broke the law. (He needed the senate's permission to bring his army so close to Rome.) The result was **civil war**. It ended in victory for Caesar, and death for Pompey.

Caesar was now the strongest man in Rome. Some Romans thought he wanted to be king. A group of them, led by **Brutus**, stabbed Caesar to death in the senate-house. The murder was followed by more civil war. (The cartoons tell the story.)

Now try Exercise 2.2.

A Caesar murdered by Brutus and others
B Antony speaks up for Caesar
C Civil war – Antony and Octavian beat Brutus and Cassius
D Antony and Octavian share the empire
E Antony falls in love with Cleopatra in Egypt
F Another civil war – Octavian beats Antony in sea battle
G Antony and Cleopatra commit suicide
H Octavian becomes emperor Augustus

Exercise 2.2

Study the cartoons, then:

Either
Write paragraph-headings for an essay telling the story. You must use your own words.
Or
Choose one of the scenes, and write a newspaper report, as if you had been there. Make up a suitable headline.

C The emperors

Augustus gave Rome peace and law and order after all the civil wars. But the senators lost their power. They had to learn to do as the emperor wished. The governors of the provinces (parts of the empire) took their orders from him. He chose the leaders of the army.

Augustus ruled Rome for 40 years. When he died, his step-son took his place. A long line of emperors followed, for more than 400 years. Sometimes, a son took over from his father. Often there were quarrels, murders, and war. As a rule, the man backed by the army got to the top.

Some emperors were wise and just. Many were cruel. Some, like Trajan, were soldiers. Others, like Hadrian, were travellers and builders. Some, like Nero, were mad. When much of Rome burnt down in AD 64, many Romans said that Nero had done it on purpose.

The empire still grew, but when Trajan conquered Dacia (see map) that was the last new gain. From now on, the army held on to what Rome had, and kept the peace. For a long time, it did this job very well. Most of western and central Europe, and all the Mediterranean lands, belonged to Rome. Everyone paid taxes to Rome and obeyed Rome's orders. The Romans called the Mediterranean 'Our Sea'.

Now try Exercise 2.3.

Exercise 2.3

Write sentences to show that you know what these words mean:

a Empire   e Senate
b Conquer   f Consul
c Civilized   g Pirates
d Barbarian   h Civil war

Sources

Students of history find out about the past from **sources**. Books, letters, and poems are **written sources**. Some books and papers are very old – we even have some that were written by Romans.

Books and papers that were written by people who were present, and saw the things they wrote about, are called **primary sources.**

Books and papers written by people who were **not** present are called **secondary sources**. The authors of secondary sources must have heard about the events from someone else, or read about them in books.

Not all sources are written. Pictures, drawings and the things found by archaeologists tell us a lot about the past.

Source **2c**

After we had won the battle, we drove Pompey's army inside its camp. I decided that we must press on and capture it. Some of his men fought bravely, but most of them were tired out by the battle, and our troops soon broke through the camp walls.

Pompey then took a horse and galloped off. About thirty of his men joined him, and they rode as hard as they could. They did not even stop at night. When they reached the coast, Pompey found a ship and set sail.

From Julius Caesar's own account of the civil war with Pompey. This battle was fought in 48 BC. Caesar was murdered in 44 BC.

Source **2d**

Augustus gave the soldiers extra pay to get them on his side. He won the people of Rome over with supplies of cheap corn. He kept the peace, and that pleased everyone. No-one dared stand against him. Rich Romans found that the wisest thing was to do as he wished.

Written in about AD 110 by the Roman author Tacitus, who was born in about AD 55, and died in AD 118. Augustus became emperor in 27 BC, and died in AD 14.

Exercise 2.4

Read **Section C**, the note on 'Sources' and **Sources 2c** and **2d**. Then answer the questions. Write your answers in the blank spaces.

a Who wrote **Source 2c**? _____

b When do you think **Source 2c** was written? Not before _____ BC, and not after _____ BC.

c Which words in **Source 2c** make you think that Caesar was present when the events happened? _____

d Is **Source 2c** a primary or a secondary source? _____

e Who wrote **Source 2d**? _____

f When was **Source 2d** written? _____

g When was the author of **Source 2d** born? _____

h When did Augustus become Roman emperor? _____

i Could the author of **Source 2d** have been there when Augustus became emperor? _____

j Is **Source 2d** a primary or a secondary source? _____

Exercise 2.5

a Look at **Sources 2a**, **2b**, **2e**, **2f**, and **2g**.
   Ask these questions about each of the sources:

   i   What is it?
   ii Where does it come from?
   iii When was it made?

   Either
   Write out the answers in five short paragraphs.
   Or
   Make a chart, with three columns for the questions, and five lines for the sources.

   If you do not know the answer to a question, write **Not known** in the box.

b Make a drawing of either **Source 2b** or **Source 2e**.

Source 2e

The Arch of Titus in Rome. It was built in about AD 80 to mark Rome's victory in the war in Palestine.

Source 2f

An aerial view of a fort made by the Roman army in Scotland in about AD 80.

Source 2g

A stone carving of a Roman ship carrying soldiers.

Source 2h

Emperor Augustus is the greatest blessing we have ever had. He is a father to us, and gives us a happy life. At land and sea, we are now at peace. In all the towns there is law and order, and plenty to eat. Men are content with what they have, and hopeful for the future.

Words carved on a stone in Asia Minor in about AD 10.

Exercise 2.6

Read **Source 2d** again, then answer these questions in sentences:

a How did Augustus get the soldiers and people of Rome on his side?
b What did Augustus do that pleased everyone?
c Why do you think rich Romans thought it was wise to do as Augustus wished?
d What makes you think that the author did not like Augustus?

Read **Source 2h**, then answer these questions in sentences:

e In one way, **Source 2h** says the same as **Source 2d**. What is that?
f Why were the people in the towns pleased with Augustus?
g Did the author of **Source 2h** think the same about Augustus as the author of **Source 2d**?

3 Roman Britain

ROMAN BRITAIN

SCOTLAND

R. Forth

R. Clyde

Antonine Wall

Corbridge

R. Tyne

NORTH SEA

Solway

Hadrian's Wall

York

IRELAND

IRISH SEA

Chester

Watling Street

WALES

St. Albans

London

Colchester

Maiden Castle

Dover

Richborough

Isle of Wight

ENGLISH CHANNEL

GAUL

0   50   100   150   200 Km

Area conquered by the Romans by AD 84

Area affected by Boudicca's revolt

A The conquest

Julius Caesar invaded Britain twice, in 55 BC and 54 BC. He may have meant to add it to Rome's empire. But revolt in Gaul made him give up the plan. Nearly a hundred years later, in AD 43, emperor **Claudius** tried again.

Claudius came to Britain himself. He stayed about two weeks. He was present when the strongest tribe in the south surrendered. He gave orders to his men to build the first Roman town in Britain — at **Colchester.** He also ordered his generals to conquer the rest of the island.

Source 3b

Left: Maiden Castle in Dorset. The centre of the 'hill fort' covers an area of 18 hectares. The earth walls are up to 6 metres high. There were wooden fences on top of the earth walls.

Above: This shows part of a man's spine, discovered at Maiden Castle. The arrowhead which killed him was fired by a Roman catapult.

Source 3a

The Romans captured the south east quite quickly. But the west, Wales, and the north gave them more trouble. So did Queen **Boudicca**, who led the revolt against the Romans in AD 60. Her followers burned Colchester and London, and killed thousands of Romans. A Roman army had to march back from north Wales to crush them.

Between AD 77 and AD 84, **Agricola** led the Romans to great success. He completed the conquest of Wales and the north. He marched into Scotland and won a great battle near Aberdeen. It looked as if the whole of Britain would soon belong to Rome.

But then Agricola returned to Rome, and the Romans changed their plans. They moved some of their troops from Britain to Germany. Now there were not enough men left to conquer Scotland, or hold on to what had been won. The Romans gave up most of Scotland and fell back to the north of England.

Now try Exercises 3.1 and 3.2.

Source 3c

In the time of Claudius, Vespasian took his legion to Britain. He conquered two of the strongest tribes. He captured more than 20 forts, and also the Isle of Wight.

Written by the Roman author Suetonius in about AD 120.

Sometimes we don't know the answers

The **Sources** tell us what we know about the past. We can learn a great deal from them. But sometimes the sources do not tell us everything we would like to know. Then we have to look for other sources, or admit that we just don't know.

Exercise 3.1

Read **Section A**, then fill in the blanks in the sentences.

a Julius Caesar came to Britain in _____ BC and _____ BC.

b Emperor _____ ordered the Romans to invade Britain in AD 43.

c The first Roman town in Britain was _____.

d The Romans had to fight hard to conquer the west and north of England, and _____.

e Queen _____ led a revolt of the British tribes against the Romans.

f Agricola was in command of the Romans in Britain for _____ years.

g Agricola won a big battle near _____ in Scotland.

h The Romans retreated from Scotland because they had not _____ _____ (two words) to hold the land they had won.

Exercise 3.2

Read **Source 3c**, and the note 'Sometimes we don't know the answers', and look at **Sources 3a and 3b**.
The sources give the answers to some but not all of the questions below. If you can find the answer to the question, write it in the space. If you cannot find it, write 'Not known'.

a Who commanded the legion which captured the hill-forts? _____

b Were there any hill-forts on the Isle of Wight? _____

c How many hill-forts did the Romans capture? _____

d Did Vespasian capture Maiden Castle? _____

e How many ditches were there around Maiden Castle? _____

f Exactly when did the Romans attack Maiden Castle? _____

g Was anyone at Maiden Castle definitely killed by a Roman? (Write a sentence, explaining your answer.) _____ _____

h Did anyone live at Maiden Castle after the Romans attacked it? _____

B Hadrian's Wall

The emperor Hadrian (AD 117–138).

In AD 122 the emperor Hadrian came to Britain. He inspected the province and ordered the army to build a wall from coast to coast. (Look at the map on page 16.) The wall was to help the Romans keep the peace. It stopped the British tribes from raiding each other. It stopped them meeting to plan revolts. It forced traders to pass through Roman gates and pay taxes to Rome.

Hadrian's Wall was 76 Roman miles (115 kilometres) long. The eastern part was stone, three metres wide and five metres high. (In the west, at first, the wall was made of earth.) Every five miles along the wall there was a **fort**, holding 500 men. Between the forts, a mile apart, were **milecastles**, with 30 to 50 men, and **turrets** for sentries.

The forts had gates opening to the north, as well as to the south. Soldiers went out on patrol, dealt with rebels and raiders, and kept in touch with the Romans to the north. For the wall was not the end of the Roman world — there were roads and a few forts beyond.

The Romans dug a **ditch** north of the wall, and a flat-bottomed ditch, called the **vallum**, behind. A road ran between the wall and the vallum. They made mounds of earth beside each ditch. Britons were not allowed in the space between the vallum and the wall, except where there were gates. The gates were at the forts, with the Roman soldiers.

Now try Exercise 3.3.

Far right: A reconstruction of a milecastle on Hadrian's Wall.

Right: A cut away reconstruction of a turret.

Below: A cross-section of Hadrian's Wall, showing the ditches, mounds, wall and road.

 N

 (a)

 (b)

 (c)

 (d)

(e)

Housesteads, a fort on Hadrian's Wall

Hadrian's Wall

C After Hadrian

Ten years after the wall was built, the Romans left it. Emperor **Antonius** sent them into Scotland again. They had to start work on a new wall, between the Forth and the Clyde — the **Antonine Wall**. This second wall was only 37 miles (60 kilometres) long. It was made of earth, and its forts were closer together than those on Hadrian's Wall.

But the Romans stayed in Scotland for only twenty years. They had to cope with wars and revolts, in front of the wall and behind. And they did not always win. They were forced to pull back into England.

In AD 208, emperor **Severus** led an army into Scotland. He beat the tribes and forced them to make peace. But he did not want the Romans to stay there. He went back to Hadrian's plan, rebuilt his forts, and made his wall longer and stronger.

There was peace in the north for a hundred years. But there was not peace elsewhere. **Saxon** pirates from north Germany began to raid the coast in about AD 250. To deal with them, the Romans built forts along the east and south coasts. And warships based in Dover tried to chase them from the sea. (See Chapter 14).

Now try Exercises 3.4 and 3.5.

Source 3d

The British tribes crossed the wall and did a lot of damage. They beat a Roman army and killed its general. The emperor (Commodus) sent Marcellus to deal with them.

Written by the Roman author Cassius Dio. He lived in Asia Minor from AD 180 to AD 229. He did not visit Britain. Commodus became Roman emperor in AD 180 and died in AD 193.

Source 3e

Early in the reign of Commodus, the barbarians to the north broke through the wall. They did a lot of damage and killed a Roman general. The source (3d) does not say which wall he meant. But there was no damage on Hadrian's wall at that time. So he must have meant the Antonine wall.

From a book written by Professor Ian Richmond in 1955. (Not Professor Richmond's own words.)

Different ideas about the past

Experts on history do not always agree with each other. Often, this is because the sources do not say enough about what happened. That is when the experts guess. And they do not all guess the same.

Source 3f

The Romans left the Antonine wall in AD 163. They fell back to the south – to Hadrian's wall. The war which the source (3d) describes took place nearly twenty years after that. So the 'wall' must have been Hadrian's wall. Also, signs of damage, done soon after AD 180, have been found at some forts on Hadrian's wall.

From a book written by Professor Sheppard Frere in 1987. (Not Professor Frere's own words.)

Note on Sources 3e and 3f

Archaeologists, as they dig, learn more and more about the Romans. The author of Source 3f knew what had been found between 1955 and 1987. He knew things that the author of Source 3e could not know.

Exercise 3.4

Read **Sources 3d**, **3e**, and **3f**, and the 'Note on Sources 3e and 3f'. Then answer the questions in sentences.

a Who wrote **Source 3d**, and when did he live?
b Did the author of **Source 3d** ever visit Britain?
c Is **Source 3d** a primary or a secondary source?
d Who wrote **Source 3e**, and when did he write it?
e **Source 3e** was written how many years after emperor Commodus died?
f Is **Source 3e** a primary or a secondary source?
g Who wrote **Source 3f**, and when did he write it?
h **Source 3f** was written how many years after **Source 3e**?
i Is **Source 3f** a primary or a secondary source?

Exercise 3.5

Read the note 'Different ideas about the past'. Discuss the questions in a group. Then answer questions **a**, **b**, and **c** in sentences, and question **d** in a paragraph.

a Something in **Source 3d** is not clear. What is it?
b How do we know that the authors of **Sources 3e** and **3f** had both read **Source 3d**?
c What difference is there between what **Sources 3e** and **3f** say?
d Can you think of any reasons why **Sources 3e** and **3f** say different things?

4 The City of Rome

A The city and its buildings

Rome was a huge city — its population was more than a million. As well as Italians, there were men and women from Greece, Spain, and Syria. The city teemed with people from all parts of the Roman world.

The forum lay at the centre of Rome. It was a large open square where Romans met to talk and do business. A market hall, law courts, and libraries stood round its edges. (You can still see their remains). Each way you looked, you saw temples, baths, arches, columns, and fountains.

Rich Romans all had homes in the city. Their houses were built round courtyards, with gardens and statues in the middle. The main rooms had glass windows and painted plaster walls. Some of them had mosaic floors. (Look at Source 4c.)

Poor families lived in one- or two-roomed apartments in brick and concrete 'insulae' or 'islands'. (We would call them blocks of flats.) Some were five or six storeys high. They had no running water, and no glass in their windows. Tallow candles were the only lights.

Now try Exercises 4.1 and 4.2.

Source **4a**

The forum. This was a place where Romans talked to their friends, heard the news, and did business deals.

Exercise 4.1

Centuries

A **century** is a period of a hundred years.
The **first century** AD was the hundred years from AD 1 to AD 100.
The **second century** AD was the hundred years from AD 101 to AD 200.
The **fifth century** AD was the hundred years from AD 401 to AD 500.
The **first century** BC was the hundred years from 100 BC to 1 BC.
Now fill in the spaces in the sentences.

a A century is a period of _____ years.

b The _____ century AD was the hundred years from AD 1 to AD 100.

c The third century AD was the hundred years from AD _____ to AD 300.

d The _____ century BC was the hundred years from 100 BC to 1 BC.

e The year AD 69 was in the _____ century AD.

f The year AD 122 was in the _____ century AD.

g The year 44 BC was in the _____ century BC.

Draw a time line from 100 BC to AD 500. Mark the dates and the names of the centuries.

Source 4c

A mosaic floor. Roman artists made pictures out of thousands of small, coloured stones and pieces of tile and glass set into concrete on the floors of rich men's homes.

Source 4d

A street in Herculaneum. This little town to the south of Rome and its neighbour, Pompeii, were destroyed when the volcano Vesuvius erupted in AD 79. Streets in Rome looked just like this, but the insulae would have been much taller.

Source 4b

This picture was painted on an inside wall of a Roman house. It shows some of the tall buildings in Rome.

Exercise 4.2

Read **Section A** and study **Sources 4a, 4b, 4c,** and **4d**. Write sentences to show that you know what these words mean:

a Population
b Forum
c Column
d Courtyard
e Mosaic
f Insulae

B Clothes and food

In Rome, a man dressed in the **toga**. It was a large piece of fine, white woollen cloth, folded and wrapped round the body. (Look at Source 4f.) The toga was a kind of uniform. (If a Roman did not wear it when he went out, people might think he was a slave.) When it was cold, he wore one or two tunics under the toga, and a cloak on top.

A Roman woman wore a tunic, and a flowing garment called a stola on top. The stola reached the ground, and was belted at the waist. She wore a cloak when she went outdoors. Her clothes were often coloured.

All Romans had enough to eat. But poor people's food was rather dull. They got cheap corn from the state, and at times it was free. The women made some of it into bread. They boiled the rest with vegetables, and some meat or fish, to make a kind of porridge.

The rich ate plenty of meat and fish, and were fond of herbs and spices. At a banquet, the guests might eat wild boar, goose, pheasant, and peacock, and very sweet cakes. (One source mentions dormice stuffed with honey!) There was always a lot of wine to drink.

Romans lay on low couches to eat. Slaves set the food on little tables in front of them. They ate with their fingers and spoons. Between courses, they wiped their hands on sponges.

Now try Exercises 4.3 and 4.4.

Source 4e

> *It's cheaper to live in the country. You only wear your toga once or twice a month. The clothes you wear for dinner parties will last ten years.*

From a Latin poem by Martial, who lived from AD 40 to AD 104.

Source 4f

This ancient Roman sculpture shows a man wearing a toga.

Exercise 4.3

Read about Roman clothes in **Section B**. Read **Source 4e**, and look at **Source 4f**. Then answer the questions.

a What was the Roman man's main garment called?
b When did Romans not wear the toga? (See **Source 4e**.)
c What was the Roman woman's main garment called?
d Mention one difference between men's and women's clothes in Rome.
e Who wrote **Source 4e**, and when?
f Would the author of **Source 4e** have seen Romans in the city and in the country?
g Is **Source 4e** a primary or a secondary source?
h Would the sculptor who made **Source 4f** have seen Roman men wearing togas?
j Is **Source 4f** a primary or a secondary source?

Source 4g

Most cooks treat dinner guests like cattle. They give them fennel, garlic, and parsley, with heaps of cabbage, beet, and spinach. It's all smothered in masses of smelly sauce and mustard. They don't give you seasoned food — they give you food that tears your insides out.

From a Latin play by Plautus, written in about 200 BC.

Source 4h

Rissoles: Grind up some pepper, lovage, and oregano, and moisten them with fish paste. Add cooked brains and five eggs, and put them in a metal pan. When this mixture is cooked, turn it out onto a board and dice. Then make the sauce with pepper, lovage, oregano, fish paste, and wine. Boil it up in a pan, and crumble in pastry to thicken. Pour the sauce over the rissoles.

From a Roman cookery book by Apicius, written in about AD 15.

A slave serving food at a religious ceremony.

Exercise 4.4

Read about Roman food in **Section B**, and read **Sources 4g** and **4h**. Write a short *essay* about Roman food, answering these questions:

i   What kind of food did the Romans like?
ii Which things did the Romans eat which we do not eat?
iii What would you have liked and disliked about Roman food?

C Daily life in Rome

Rich Romans did not have to work for a living. Their money came from their estates — the land they owned outside Rome. The poorest did not work much either. They lived mainly on hand-outs of cheap corn, and on what they could beg from their richer friends.

The hardest workers in Rome were the craftsmen and traders. The narrow streets were full of their little shops. You could buy most things in Rome — fruit, fish, wine, shoes, clothes, rare spices, and the finest glass vases. The shops opened straight onto the streets. The craftsmen worked in the front rooms, and their families lived in the back.

This is a carving of a Roman butcher chopping up meat.

Work in Rome began at dawn, but ended soon after mid-day. There were no week-ends, but plenty of 'feast days', when no-one worked.

Rome was not a healthy place. The sewers got rid of the rain-water, but refuse lay in the streets. The Romans were proud of the **aqueducts** that brought fresh water from the hills, but few houses had water on tap. The poor had to carry water from the public fountains.

Disease was common. Doctors did not know much, and often did more harm than good. (Only the rich could afford doctors, in any case.) Most Romans bought herbs, ointments, and miracle cures in the drug shops. A few of these treatments worked, many did not, and some were deadly.

The streets were always noisy and cluttered. Shopkeepers set out their goods on the pavement, and sellers of hot pies and sausages passed up and down, shouting above the din. No wheeled carts were allowed in the streets in the day-time. So they rumbled up and down all night.

Now try Exercise 4.5.

Source **4i**

There are often fires in the middle of the night. And if you live in a third-floor flat you're in real danger. By the time the smoke wakes you, your neighbours below have moved to safety. The last to fry is the one in the attic, who lives up among the pigeons.

It's risky to walk in the streets at night. A tile falling from a roof could brain you. You might be hit by a cracked pot that someone throws out of his window. Or a housewife might drop a bucket of slops on your head. Then there's the drunken bully who will beat you up, or the thief with his knife. Rich men go about with their bodyguards, but the poor have to take their chance.

From a Latin poem by Juvenal, who lived from AD 55 to AD 140.

Source **4j**

Two of my houses have fallen down. In the others, the walls are all cracked. Not only the tenants have left — the mice have gone as well.

Part of a letter written by Cicero, who lived from 106 BC to 43 BC.

Exercise 4.5

Read **Section C**, and read **Sources 4i** and **4j**.

Do you agree with the following statement?

Even poor Romans had plenty to eat and lived an easy life.

  i Find reasons for **agreeing** with the statement.
  ii Find reasons for **disagreeing** with the statement.
  (You might find it useful to have a discussion in a group.)

Then do one of the following:

a Write down what you think in *two* paragraphs.
b Make a chart, with *two* columns — reasons for agreeing and reasons for disagreeing.
c Make notes so that you can give a short talk to the rest of the class.
d Draw cartoons to show some good and bad things about living in Rome.

5 The Roman Army

A Rome's soldiers

The army conquered the empire, and made Rome great. And the army kept her great. It fought off Rome's enemies, such as the Persians and the Germans. It was also a police force. It dealt with rebels and bandits, and gave peace to Rome's subjects.

Rome's **legions** were its first-class troops. A legion was a force of 5,000 foot-soldiers. It was commanded by a **legate**. It was divided into **cohorts** of about 500 men, and **centuries** of 80 men. The officer in charge of a century was called a **centurion**.

Up to about AD 100 the legions were made up of men from Italy. Some, but not many, would be from Rome itself. Young men between 18 and 22 were keen to join up, for the pay was good.

Source 5a

This carving on Trajan's column shows soldiers crossing a bridge of boats. The standard-bearers are in front. The soldiers have their helmets on their right shoulders (carved about AD 110).

Source 5b

This carving from Rome shows an emperor speaking to men from the legions. You can see their 'eagles' above their heads. The carving was made in AD 315.

Each man thought his own legion was the best, and would die to save its **eagle**. The eagle was the legion's standard. It was a bronze bird on a pole, which was carried into battle in front of the troops. The legion was disgraced if the enemy captured its eagle.

The second-class troops were called **auxiliaries**. They were from the provinces of the empire, such as Gaul or Spain. They served with men from their own country, but their officers were Roman. All the commands were in Latin, and they had to learn to fight like Romans. They fought in **cohorts** of 500 or 1000 men. All of Rome's special troops (such as archers, slingers, and cavalry) were auxiliaries.

Now try Exercise 5.1.

B Ready for war

The Romans won most of their wars. The main reason was that their soldiers were well trained. They could march, turn, advance, or retreat together, always in good order. The men were fit and tough. They trained with armour and weapons that were twice as heavy as those they used in war.

Romans did a lot of marching. A day's march was 30 kilometres in five hours. Then they had to build a camp. They dug ditches, piled up earth walls, and set a wooden fence on top. They pitched their leather tents inside.

A trumpet call at dawn next day told them to take down the tents and pile the baggage on the mules. They lined up in ranks, and the legate shouted, 'Romans, are you ready for war?'. The men replied, 'We are ready'.

Now try Exercises 5.2 and 5.3.

Exercise 5.1

a Read **section A**, then write the meanings of these words.
i	Legion	**v**	Eagle
ii	Cohort	**vi**	Auxiliaries
iii	Century	**vii**	Cavalry
iv	Centurion		

b Draw a Roman soldier (see illustrations).

Source 5c

A Roman helmet. On special parades they would wear a plume of feathers fixed to the top.

Exercise 5.2

Read **Section B** and **Source 5d**. Look at the picture sources (**Sources 5a, 5b,** and **5c**). Write the answers to the questions in the spaces.

a Which weapons can you see in the picture sources?

_____

b **Source 5d** says Roman soldiers carried what weapons?

_____

c Does **Source 5d** say the same as the picture sources about weapons?

_____

d Do the picture sources all say the same about Roman helmets? _____

e **Source 5d** says that armour covered which parts of a soldier's body?

_____

f Do the picture sources say the same as **Source 5d** about armour? _____

g What does **Source 5d** say about the shape of Roman shields? _____

h Which picture source agrees with **Source 5d** about the shape of shields, and which disagrees? _____

_____

Exercise 5.3

Read the note 'Can we trust the sources?', then answer the questions in sentences.

a When and where did Josephus (the author of **Source 5d**) live? Would he have seen Roman soldiers?

b Should we believe what Josephus tells us about Roman soldiers?

c **Sources 5a** and **5b** were made when and where? Would the sculptors have seen Roman soldiers?

d Should we believe what the picture sources tell us about soldiers?

e Why should we believe what **Source 5c** tells us about helmets?

f Can you think of a reason why the sources do not all say the same about soldiers' arms and equipment?

Can we trust the sources?

Things that are written are not bound to be true. Some authors make mistakes. Some authors make stories up, or leave important events out. The same can be true of artists and sculptors.

If an author, or artist, was present and saw or heard what was happening, then what he tells us is more likely to be true.

Source **5d**

Foot-soldiers are armed with a cuirass and a helmet. They carry two swords, one on each side. The one on the left is much longer than the other. They carry a spear and a tall oblong shield. Also, they carry a saw, a basket, a pick, an axe, and enough rations for three days.

Written by a Jewish writer called Josephus. He lived in the first century AD, and wrote about the wars between the Jews and the Romans which took place in his time.

(A cuirass is a piece of armour covering the chest and the top of the back.)

A bronze statue of a legionary, made in the second century AD. On top he wears a cuirass. Below he wears a kilt of strips of leather plated with metal.

C Service in the army

When not at war, the soldiers lived in forts, with stone walls, paved streets, and solid buildings. (Look at the plan.) A legion's fort was like a small town. Villages grew up outside the forts, with shops and inns. There was always someone to help the soldiers spend their money.

Roman soldiers had to be builders and engineers as well as fighters. A legion built its own roads and bridges. Its craftsmen repaired its armour and weapons. It even made its own cooking-pots and roof tiles.

Compared with most people of their time, Roman soldiers ate well. They got a ration of pork fat and barley each day, with extra meat and vegetables if they were lucky. The men did their own cooking. They sometimes made bread, but more often they had a kind of stew.

Until about AD 200, soldiers were not allowed to marry while they were in the army. (Officers were allowed to marry.) At the end of their 25 years service, though, they were given a sum of money and some land. Many of them married then, and settled down as farmers. Some went to **colonies** — special towns for ex-soldiers. Others lived and died near the forts where they had served.

To the spirits of the departed. Julius Valens, former soldier of the Second Legion, lived 100 years. Julia, his wife, and Martinus, her son, set this up.

(Words carved on a tombstone found near Caerleon fortress in south Wales. Julius was probably about 45 years old when he left the army.)

Now try Exercises 5.4 and 5.5.

Causes and Reasons

A **cause** is a reason for something. It is the answer to the question '**Why** did it happen?'. For example, **Why** was Julius Caesar murdered?

Often, there is more than one answer to the question 'Why?' There is more than one **cause** for most things.

Source 5e

The Romans never stop training. Their peace-time exercises are just as hard as real battles. That is why they are never afraid in war, and never get tired out.

From the book of Josephus (see Source 5d).

A plan of a typical Roman Fort.

Source 5f

The barbarians yelled and chanted. But the Romans marched on in silence. When the two sides were close, a sign was made. The Roman legion rushed forward. They broke through the first line, but there were still great numbers of the enemy. The archers then dealt with the enemy chariots, and the cavalry scattered the men on foot.

Written by the Roman historian Cassius Dio, about a battle in Britain.

Source 5g

From Claudia to Lepidina. I hope you will come to my birthday party on 11 September. You will make us happy if you are there.

These words were written in Latin on a thin piece of wood, which was found at the Vindolanda camp in the north of England. Archaeologists know, from where it was found, that it was written in about AD 100. Claudia and Lepidina are women's names.

Source 5h

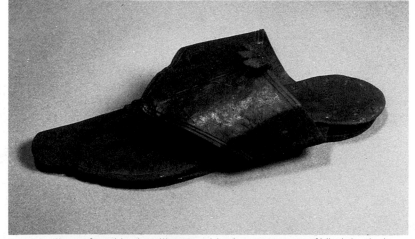

A lady's slipper found in the village outside the army camp of Vindolanda. It was made in about AD 100. The maker's name (Thales) was marked on the bottom of the shoe.

Exercise 5.4

Read the note on 'Causes and Reasons', and read **Sources 5e** and **5f**.

Why did the Romans win most of their battles? What were the **causes** of the victories? Discuss these questions in a group. (You will find some causes in Section B, and some in Sources 5e and 5f.)

Either **a**) Make a group tape giving your answers or **b**) Make a wall display, with pictures and pieces of written work.

Exercise 5.5

Read **Source 5g** and look at **Source 5h**. Which of these questions can we answer?

Write down:
  i   Answers for the questions we can answer.
  ii 'Not known' for the questions we cannot answer.

a How do we know Claudia's and Lepidina's names?
b How do we know that Claudia and Lepidina were Romans?
c Where and when did Claudia and Lepidina live?
d Who were Claudia's and Lepidina's husbands?
e How do we know that Claudia and Lepidina could read and write?
f What kind of shoe was **Source 5h**?
g Who made **Source 5h**, and when?
h How much did **Source 5h** cost?
j Who owned **Source 5h**?

6 The Countryside

A Country estates in Italy and Britain

One hundred million people lived in the Roman empire. Most of them were **peasants**, or workers on the land. They grew corn, and kept cattle, sheep, pigs, and goats. (In Italy, they grew olives and vines as well.) And they kept bees for honey – the Romans had no sugar.

The peasants did not own the land. In Italy, it belonged to the rich Romans. Their **estates** earned them the money they spent in Rome. They came out from time to time to stay in their villas (country houses). In Britain, local chiefs or nobles owned the land. They too had houses in the towns, and villas in the country.

Peasants paid rent to the landlord. Often, it was not in money. Instead, they paid their landlords so much corn, or so many cattle or sheep each year. When the landlord was away in town, his **bailiff** collected the rents, and saw that all was well.

On some estates in Italy, there were no peasants. Instead, there were gangs of slaves. On these estates the bailiff's job was to make the slaves work, and make sure that they did not run away. Peasants hated landlords who used slaves – it meant no land and no work for the peasants.

Now try Exercises 6.1. and 6.2.

Source 6a

The carving (from a landowner's tomb) shows peasants giving presents to their landlord. As well as paying rent they had to bring gifts at certain times of the year.

Exercise 6.1

Read **Section A**, then write down the meanings of these words.

a Peasant　　d Rent
b Estate　　e Landlord
c Villa　　f Bailiff

Source 6b

Peasants' lives are peaceful, honest, and secure. They work hard, but they work for themselves. They live in cool valleys, beside rivers and lakes. They can sleep in the shade of tall green trees, or go hunting in woods full of game.

From a poem by Virgil. He lived for part of his life on his father's estate in northern Italy, and spent some years in Rome.

Source 6c

The hillsides are covered with vines. Beyond them are the meadows and cornfields. All the fields are watered by streams that never run dry. The river Tiber runs through the valley. In winter and spring it is wide and deep enough to take the ships that carry my farm produce to Rome. In summer the water-level falls, but it fills up in the autumn.

From a letter by Pliny, written in about AD 105.

Exercise 6.2

Study **Source 6a** and read **Sources 6b** and **6c**. Then answer the questions.

a Look at **Source 6a**. Can you make out what presents the peasants are giving their landlord? Write down what you think the presents are. Here are some suggestions to help:

a young goat　a jar of wine　two fish　a young pig　a lamb　a set of bagpipes　a basket of fruit　an eel　a hare　a hen

Peasant 1 ＿＿＿＿　Peasant 3 ＿＿＿＿　Peasant 5 ＿＿＿＿
Peasant 2 ＿＿＿＿　Peasant 4 ＿＿＿＿　Peasant 6 ＿＿＿＿

b Is **Source 6a** a primary or a secondary source? (Write a sentence, giving your reasons.)

c Which two crops do we know grew on Pliny's estate (**Source 6c**)? ＿＿＿＿

d Which words in **Source 6c** prove that summers were dry and hot in Italy?

e Is **Source 6c** a primary or a secondary source? (Write a sentence, giving your reasons.)

f Was Virgil (**Source 6b**) a peasant? Would he know how peasants lived? ＿＿＿＿

g Did Virgil think it was better to live in the country or in Rome? ＿＿＿＿

h Is **Source 6b** a primary or a secondary source? (Write a sentence, giving your reasons.)

B Villas

Some estates near Rome and in the south of Italy were huge. The richest Romans kept thousands of slaves to work their land. Others, such as Virgil's father's estate (see Source 6b), were quite small. British chiefs owned far less land than the great men of Rome.

Villas varied also — the bigger the estate, the bigger and grander the villa.

Near Rome and round the Bay of Naples were villas with dozens of rooms, glass windows, and painted walls. Their mosaic floors showed country scenes or told stories of the gods and heroes. They were built round gardens, with fountains, ponds, and statues in the middle. (Look at Source 6d). Every villa had its own bath house.

Source 6d

This copy of a Roman villa has been built in America. The real villa was destroyed when the volcano Vesuvius erupted in AD 79.

Source 6e

This mosaic was found in one of the rooms of Fishbourne Palace in Sussex. Fishbourne was built in about AD 70. It was burned down between AD 250 and 300.

Villas in Britain, at first, were far smaller. But by the fourth century AD, some of them were copies of Italy's best. Being farther north, they were colder. So they had **hypocausts**, or central heating, in some rooms in the house, not just in the baths. (Look at Source 6f).

Roman estate-owners liked to go to their villas in the summer. It was much cooler there than in Rome, there was less noise, and they did not have to wear their togas. Also, they could go hunting, their favourite sport. British landlords were the same — they too spent part of the year in town, and part in the country.

Now try Exercise 6.3.

Source **6f**

A hypocaust from Fishbourne palace. A furnace heated the air, which then passed through channels under the floor and warmed the room from below. Paving stones were laid over the channels, with perhaps a mosaic on top of them.

Exercise 6.3

Read **Section B** and study **Sources 6d, 6e,** and **6f**. Fill in the missing words in the sentences.

a The biggest estates were near _____ and in the _____ of Italy.

b The finest villas had _____ windows, _____ walls, and _____ on the floors.

c All big villas had their own _____ houses.

d The volcano Vesuvius (see **Source 6d**) erupted in the _____ century AD.

e Fishbourne palace (see **Source 6e**) was built in the _____ century AD, and was burned down in the _____ century AD.

f In a _____ (see **Source 6f**), the heat came from hot _____ in channels under the floor.

Draw a time line from AD 1 to AD 400. Mark the centuries and as many facts as possible from Sources **6d, 6e** and **6f**.

C The peasants and the state

Was rule by Rome good or bad for peasants? Many of them no doubt grumbled. And they had a good deal to grumble about. They not only had to pay rent to their landlords, but taxes to the state as well. They were also made to work, without pay, on the roads to keep them in repair.

In Britain, the peasants were forced to sell corn to the army, at a price the Romans fixed. The peasants complained that the corn price was too low, but they probably did quite well from the trade. At least they knew they could sell their corn.

The army was also a good customer for peasants who kept cattle. Soldiers ate the meat, and made leather from the skins. And there were a hundred uses for leather in the Roman army —

such as boots, shields, armour-straps, tents, horses' harness, etc.

The best thing for peasants about Roman rule was **peace**. Before the Romans came, tribes were often at war. Peasants could be killed, or captured and sold as slaves. Even when there was no war, bandits might come at any time and steal the cattle. The Romans ended the wars, built roads, stopped cattle raiding, and gave Britain law and order.

Now try Exercises 6.4 and 6.5.

Source 6g

There are lots of people and cattle in Britain. The most civilized part is Kent, where the people are the same as the Gauls. Most of the others do not grow grain. They live on meat and milk. They dress in skins.

Written by Julius Caesar, who came to Britain with an army in 55 BC and 54 BC. He advanced through the south-east of England, but did not stay.

Source 6h

The men of Britain live like the Gauls, but are not so civilized. They have plenty of milk, but don't know how to make cheese. They know nothing about growing crops.

Written by Strabo in about AD 10 (before the Romans conquered Britain). Strabo never visited Britain himself.

Causes and results

Causes come **before** events. They are the reasons why they happen. A quarrel about Sicily was the cause of the war between Rome and Carthage.

Results come **after** events. One result of the war between Rome and Carthage was that the coast of Spain became part of the Roman empire.

What the archaeologists tell us

Before the Romans came all the Britons grew corn. Most of them wore clothes made from woollen cloth. They were civilized in some ways – their craftsmen made beautiful gold ornaments. The most advanced Britons lived in Kent and other parts of the south-east. There were no cities.

Exercise 6.4

Read Section C, and the notes on 'Causes and results'. What were the **results** for peasants of being ruled by Rome?

a Make your own notes, **or** make a chart. Separate your notes or chart into
  i Results that were bad for the peasants, and
  ii Results that were good for the peasants.
b Draw a cartoon to show one of the results of Roman rule.

Exercise 6.5

Read Sources **6g** and **6h** and 'What the archaeologists tell us'. Answer questions **a** to **f** in sentences, and question **g** in a paragraph.

a Who wrote **Source 6g**, and when?
b Did the author of **Source 6g** ever visit Britain?
c Who wrote **Source 6h**, and when?
d Did the author of **Source 6h** ever visit Britain?
e Compare **Source 6g** with 'What the archaeologists tell us'.
  i What did **Source 6g** get right?
  ii What did **Source 6g** get wrong?
f Compare **Source 6h** with 'What the archaeologists tell us'. What did **Source 6h** get wrong?
g Can you think of any **reasons** why Sources **6g** and **6h** got some things wrong?

7 Towns and Trade

TOWNS AND ROADS IN ROMAN BRITAIN

SCOTLAND
Carlisle
Dere Street
IRISH SEA
Aldborough
York
NORTH SEA
Chester
Lincoln
Ermine Street
Wroxeter
Leicester
WALES
Watling Street
Caister-by-Norwich
Caerwent
Caerleon
Cirencester
St. Albans
Colchester
Fosse Way
Silchester
London
Winchester
Canterbury
Richborough
Exeter
Chichester
ENGLISH CHANNEL

0 50 100 150 200 Km

- ■ Towns over 95 hectares in area
- ⊙ Towns between 45 and 95 hectares
- • Towns of less than 45 hectares

Towns and roads in Roman Britain. No one knows how many people lived in the Roman towns in Britain. The towns with the biggest area probably contained the most people. Towns in Roman Britain were much smaller than Rome and the other big cities round the Mediterranean.

A Towns

Romans thought that people were either **civilized** or they were **barbarians**. Civilized people, such as the Romans and Greeks, lived in towns. They went to meetings in the town hall, and served on juries in the law courts. They bought their food in the shops. They relaxed by going to the public baths and the theatre.

Barbarians, such as the Gauls and Britons, lived in villages, or in woods and forests. So when the Romans conquered Gaul and Britain, they set out to build towns. They got the chiefs to use the baths and wear the toga. They taught the chiefs' sons to speak Latin. Before long, the leading men in Gaul and Britain had town houses and villas in the country.

The towns were copies of Rome. Each had a forum, with the town hall and law courts on one side. The other three sides were lined with shops. Often there was a shady arcade, with columns, in front of the shops. There were paved streets, public baths, temples, and a theatre. But it was all on a smaller scale than in Rome. There were no high 'insulae', or blocks of flats.

With the towns came the merchants. They were traders — buyers and sellers of cloth, pots, spices, and wine. Merchants from Greece and Syria turned up in every town in the empire. Some were as rich as chiefs and senators.

Now try Exercise 7.1.

Exercise 7.1

Read **Section A** and study the Map. Write the names of the towns in the blank spaces in the chart.

Towns over 95 hectares	Towns between 45 and 95 hectares	Towns under 45 hectares	
....	....	....	....
....	....	....	....
	....	....	....
		....	....
		....	....
		....	....

B Industry

Towns were full of craftsmen, working in their little shops, and selling the goods they made. Leather workers made shoes and belts and harness. Metal workers made lamps and buckles and brooches. Goldsmiths made jewellery for the rich. In the biggest towns, you could even find wall-painters, sculptors and mosaic-makers.

Every Roman town had its tailors and dressmakers. But the woollen cloth (and most clothes were made of wool) was made in the countryside. There were estates where they kept great flocks of sheep, mainly for the wool. It was the job of peasant women to spin yarn, using a **spindle** and **distaff**. A **weaver** then wove the yarn, or thread, to make cloth.

The Romans used pots for everything. They stored food in them, they cooked in them, they carried water in them. Merchant-ships carried cargoes of corn, wine, olive oil, and shell-fish in large earthen jars called 'amphorae'. All these pots broke easily, so there must have been a lot of pottery-makers.

A carving showing workmen in a workshop.

37

On every Roman site, archaeologists find scraps of **pottery**. (Sometimes, but not often, they find whole pots.) They can tell, from a small piece, where it was made, and when. They know that there were pot-making factories in Italy, in Gaul, and in Britain. They know that there were shops selling new ones in every town.

Spain and Britain were important to the Romans for the metals they produced. Tin and copper were mined in Spain. Lead was mined in Britain — in Somerset, Derbyshire, and Yorkshire. There were tin mines in Cornwall. Iron ore came from Kent and the Forest of Dean.

The Romans even mined coal when they found it near the surface. (There were no deep pits.) In most homes they still burned wood, but there were a few villas where they used coal in the bathhouse furnace. At least one army camp in the north had a store of coal.

Now try Exercise 7.2.

A wine merchant's sign from Pompeii. The two men are carrying an amphora.

Exercise 7.2

Read **Section B**.
a After each of the sentences below, write TRUE or FALSE.

i   Roman craftsmen all worked in big factories. _____

ii   Most Romans wore woollen clothes. _____

iii Roman women all made their own dresses. _____

iv   Peasant women used the distaff and spindle. _____

v   Romans cooked in earthen pots instead of metal pans. _____

vi   Corn was carried in earthen jars called 'amphorae'. _____

vii No Roman pottery was made in Britain. _____

viii Britain was important to the Romans for lead, tin, and iron. _____

ix   Most villas in Roman Britain had coal fires. _____

b Draw a picture showing how a full amphora was carried.

C Travellers

Every part of the Roman empire had a network of **roads**. They were built for the army. Soldiers marched on them to get quickly from place to place. Ox-drawn carts used them to carry loads of food and supplies.

There was a Roman **post service**. It did not take letters and parcels, but was for the emperor's messengers. Towns and forts along the way had hotels where the messengers could rest and change their horses. There was also a kind of traffic police. Patrols of soldiers kept watch for bandits. Any they caught were put to death.

Slow wagons, pulled by oxen or mules, carried merchants' goods from town to town. But merchants did most of their trade by sea. Ships sailed for Rome with cargoes of corn, wine, olive oil, spices, and metals from all parts of the Mediterranean.

All trade with Britain had to travel by sea, of course. London and Richborough, in Kent, were the main ports. Ship loads of wine, oil, and the fish paste that the Romans liked were coming in all the time. They returned laden with corn, lead, and tin. A main road ran through Kent. And from London, roads fanned out to all parts of Roman Britain.

Now try Exercise 7.3.

Source 7a

I had five ships built, and got a cargo of wine, and sent them off for Rome. Every one was wrecked. But I did not lose heart, and my wife stood by me. She sold all her jewellery and most of her clothes. I got another cargo of wine, bacon, beans, perfume, and slaves. I made ten million on the voyage. I bought some land, slaves, and cattle, and built myself a country villa.

From a story made up by a Roman called Petronius in about AD 60. These words are spoken by a character called Trimalchio. Petronius was never a merchant. But he must have travelled by sea at times.

Source 7b

The merchant who overloads his ship must be mad. He piles on the cargo, then sets sail, even when a storm is blowing up. Why does he do it? For money, of course.

But before the night is over, the poor fool finds himself in the water, with his purse in this teeth. His ship and cargo are lost. He will end his days in rags, begging for a few coppers and a crust of bread.

From a Latin poem by Juvenal, written in about AD 120. He was not writing about a real person. He was warning what can happen to greedy merchants. Like Petronius, Juvenal had travelled by sea.

Exercise 7.3

Read **Section C** and **Sources 7a** and **7b**. Answer the questions in sentences.

a Who wrote **Source 7a**, and when?
b Who spoke in **Source 7a**? Was he a real person?
c Is **Source 7a** fact or fiction?
d How did the author of **Source 7a** know what it was like to travel by sea in Roman times?
e Do you think there were merchants like Trimalchio in the Roman empire?
f Who wrote **Source 7b**, and when?
g Does **Source 7b** describe a real merchant?
h How did the author of **Source 7b** know what it was like to travel by sea in Roman times?

Roman merchant ships in the harbour of Stabiae.

Different points of view

People with different **points of view** do not see things in quite the same way. A farmer might be glad when it rains – it helps the crops to grow. But someone on holiday would not have the same **point of view.**

Caesar's friends were happy when he beat Pompey in the civil war. But Pompey's friends were sad – they had a different **point of view.**

Source 7c

A aerial view of Richborough. You can see the ditches round most of the Roman Fort. On the left you can see the River Stour and the railway. The Roman harbour buildings were destroyed when the railway was built, about a hundred years ago.

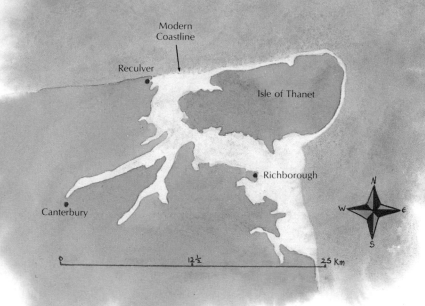

North-east Kent in the time of the Romans. The map shows that Richborough was on the coast and that Thanet was a real island. Scraps of amphorae which once contained oil, wine, olives, and fruit from Gaul, have been found at Richborough.

Missing evidence

Written sources, old buildings, coins, pots, etc., all tell us things about the Romans. We call what we learn from the sources **evidence.** Sometimes, there is not as much evidence as we would like. Old books and papers have been lost. Old buildings have been pulled down. Scraps of pottery have been thrown away. We have to try to understand the past by using the evidence that does remain.

8 Technology

A Builders and engineers

Technology means knowing how to do a job – having the right tools and knowledge. The Romans did some jobs very well. We can still see signs of the great skill of their builders and engineers.

The halls, temples, and arches in their cities show what fine builders the Romans were. They did not invent the **arch**, but it was the key to most of what they did. Using the arch, door-ways could be bigger and grander than before. Arches led to the **vault**, a way of building a high, wide roof. And the vault led to the **dome**. (Look at Source 8a). This meant they could have a large, round hall, with no columns in the middle.

The Romans built mainly in stone. So they had to solve the problem of how to cut, lift, and move large blocks of stone. (Look at Source 8b). But not

Source 8a

Inside the dome of the Pantheon, a temple in Rome.

Source 8b

A crane for lifting heavy stones. Power was supplied by the slaves inside the treadmill.

all their buildings were stone. They also used brick, and they even invented a kind of concrete.

They were planners and engineers as well as builders. All their towns had supplies of fresh water. It ran in pipes and channels, often for miles, sometimes on great **aqueducts** over valleys. Builders of water-channels could make no mistakes — the water had to flow gently downhill all the way.

The Romans solved the problems they needed to solve. But they did not see the need for some things that we take for granted. They did not invent many machines. They did not think they needed them, for they had plenty of slaves. They knew that a water-wheel could work a flourmill, but most of their mills were worked by donkeys and slaves.

Now try Exercise 8.1.

Source 8c

The Pont du Gard, an aqueduct in southern Gaul.

Exercise 8.1

Read **Section A**, and look at **Sources 8b** and **8c**. Write down *six* problems the Roman engineers and builders had to solve when they were planning and building the aqueduct in **Source 8c**.

B Road makers

Wherever it went, the army built roads. The roads were meant to stand up to hard wear, floods, and frosts. They lasted for hundreds of years, and some of them can still be seen today.

Army engineers decided where to build the roads. On dry land that was not too hilly, they followed straight lines. They got their scouts to put up markers (tall posts or bonfires) on hilltops and other high points. Then they told the road-makers to work from one marker to the next.

There was a set way of making a road. There was always a ditch at either side, so that the road would not get flooded. Then there had to be firm foundations, such as large broken stones. Above this came three or four levels of gravel and clay, packed down hard. The surface was solid stones, fitted together closely and smooth on top.

From one end of the empire to the other, you could travel on Roman roads. They crossed rivers and gorges on arched stone bridges. In hilly country, they had lots of bends, so as not to be too steep. Sometimes they ran in cuttings or tunnels through solid rock.

Now try Exercise 8.2.

Motives

Students of history often try to work out the **motives** of the people in the past. A **motive** is a **reason** for an action. When we ask, 'What were a person's motives?' we mean, 'What was he trying to do?' or, 'Why did he act as he did?'

Source 8d

> *The first stage is to dig ditches. Then they make a trench in the soil between the ditches. The trench is filled up with a foundation course, then a watertight layer. Then they lay another foundation course for the roadway. The foundation must not be loose, or the road will not be firm. The roadway is made with pointed blocks, held in place by wedges.*

Written by the Roman author Statius in about AD 90.

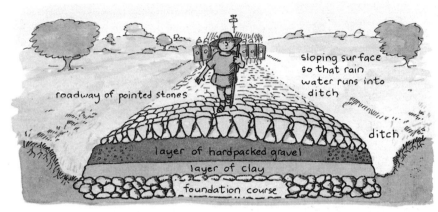

A cross-section of a Roman road.

Exercise 8.2

Read **Section B, Source 8d**, and the note on **Motives**. What do you think were the **motives** of the Roman road-builders?

Some of the sentences below are right, and some are wrong. Write TRUE or FALSE in the spaces after the sentences.

a They wanted to make good roads so that Roman soldiers could march quickly from place to place. _____

b They made a lot of roads because they wanted to give work to the local people. _____

c They needed to build good roads to carry the wagons that took food to the Roman armies. _____

d They made the roads straight so that men and supplies could travel as quickly as possible. _____

e They dug ditches so that the roads would not get flooded in wet weather. _____

f They made cuttings and tunnels so that the enemy would not see the Roman soldiers. _____

Copy the drawing of a cross-section of a Roman road.

Roman glassware, made in the first century AD and found in Radnage, England.

C **Craftsmen**

As you read in Chapter 7, every Roman town contained the workshops of craftsmen. In museums we can see the knives, brooches, pots, vases and other objects that they made. So we know that their technology was advanced.

Sources 8f, and 8h prove the skill of Roman metal-workers. But before the time of the Roman empire, the Greeks and Syrians had known just as much. Some of the finest craftsmen in Rome came from the east. But it was not only in the east that there were clever metal-workers. Source 8g was made in Britain **before** the Romans came.

Roman potters were also very skil-ful. They made pots and jars of all sizes and shapes. Some were plain, some were painted, some had patterns and pictures on the clay. The best pottery was **glazed** – dark and shiny. But potters before the Romans knew how to use the potter's wheel, and how to make glazed ware.

Rich Romans had glass vases and jugs in their homes. (Look at Source 8e.) They had glass windows which let the light in, although you could hardly see through them. The technology of glass-making came to Rome from Syria. Syrian glass-makers settled in Rome. Others moved on to Gaul and Spain, and even to Britain. From them, local craftsmen learned the skill.

Now attempt Exercise 8.3.

Source 8f

A silver dish (60cm across) made by a Roman craftsman. It was found in Suffolk.

Source 8h

A bronze lamp in the shape of a dog's head.

Source 8g

A gold brooch for fastening clothes. It was made by British craftsmen before the Romans arrived. It was found in Snettisham, Norfolk.

Exercise 8.3

Read **Section C**, and look at **Sources 8e, 8f, 8g,** and **8h.**

Decide what each picture shows, what the object was made from, and where it was found. Fill in the answers in the chart. If you cannot find the answer, write 'Not known'.

Source	What is it?	What is it made from?	Where was it found?
8e	....	....	....
8f	....	....	....
8g	....	....	....
8h	....	....	....

Source **8i**

To the emperor Hadrian, father of his country, in the fourth year of his reign. From Leicester, 2 miles.

Carved on a milestone near Leicester. The first year of Hadrian's reign was AD 117.

Source **8j**

To the emperor Hadrian, father of his country, in the fifth year of his reign. From Canovium, 8 miles.

Carved on a milestone near Conwy in north Wales.

Source **8k**

To the emperor ... From Navio, 11 miles.

Carved on a milestone near Buxton. Navio was Brough in Derbyshire.

Source **8l**

To the god of roads and paths. Titus Irdas kept his promise and built this altar.

Carved on an altar found at Catterick in Yorkshire.

Exercise 8.4

Read **Sources 8i, 8j, 8k** and **8l**. Answer the questions in sentences.

a How can we work out when **Source 8i** was carved?
b In which year was **Source 8i** carved?
c In which year was **Source 8j** carved?
d In which century were **Sources 8i** and **8j** carved?
e We do not know when **Source 8k** was carved. Which two facts are missing?
f Who set up **Source 8l**?
g Why do we not know when **Source 8l** was set up?
h How is **Source 8l** different from **Sources 8i, 8j,** and **8k**?

9 Slavery

Source 9a

A chain which was used by the Britons to stop slaves from running away. It was found in Anglesey.

Source 9b

A bronze tag worn by a slave. It says 'If I run away, hold me. Return me to my master Viventius, on the estate of Callistus'.

A Slaves' work

In all parts of the ancient world there were slaves. In Egypt and Greece, they thought it was quite normal for men and women to be **owned** by others. Therefore, it would have been strange if the Romans had not used slaves.

A lot of slaves worked on rich Romans' estates. (See Chapter 6.) They were sometimes kept chained together, day and night. The bailiff in charge might himself be a trusted slave. The work was hard and the hours were long. It was cold in the winter, and too hot in the summer. And bailiffs were always ready to use the whip.

House-slaves were better off. They

House-slave arranging a lady's hair.

cooked, cleaned, and waited at table in the houses of the rich. Ladies had squads of slave-girls to wash and dress them and do their hair. Some families kept clever Greek slaves as doctors, or teachers for their children. All house-slaves knew that if they were lazy or cheeky they would be sent to work in the fields.

Shopkeepers and craftsmen had one or two slaves, as labourers and servants in the house. A few were lucky enough to own slaves who were skilled workers. (Some of the best jewellers in Rome were slaves.) And booksellers kept slaves who could read and write – to copy out books.

Not all Romans owned slaves. The poorest families in Rome and most peasants in the country had none. Slaves were expensive to buy. And if you bought a slave, you had to feed and clothe him. If you did not, he would die, and that would be a waste of money.

Now try Exercise 9.1.

Exercise 9.1

Read **Section A** and look at **Source 9a**, then complete the sentences below by writing words in the blank spaces.

a They had slaves in Greece and _____ as well as Rome.

b The man in charge of the slaves on an estate was called the _____

c Slaves on the estates were chained together to stop them _____

d Rich Romans had slaves in their homes to do the _____ -work.

e Most house-slaves were _____ and worked hard because they did not want to be sent to the _____

f Clever Greek slaves worked as _____ or _____ in some Roman homes.

g Booksellers kept slaves who could _____ and _____ to copy out books by _____

h The poorest Romans could not _____ to buy and keep slaves.

B Slaves and the law

The law said that slaves belonged to their masters, just like cattle or sheep. So masters could buy and sell slaves as they chose. There were kind masters, who kept families of slaves together, but they did not have to do so. There was many a scene of heartbreak in the slave market as mothers were parted from their children.

If slaves did wrong, their masters could punish them as they wished. For example they could flog them, or send them to work in the fields. Until about AD 120, masters could even have their slaves put to death. But most Romans said that it was stupid to kill your own

Source **9c**

A good slave can be trusted to look after his master's business. He does a good job whether his master's there or not. He thinks about his own back – he'll get a good flogging if he's lazy. So I've decided to be a good slave. I'll do as my master says, and always be there when he wants me. It won't be long before he gives me a reward for good service.

From a play by Plautus, written in about 200 BC. This is part of a speech by a slave called Messenio. Plautus was not a slave, but he may have owned slaves.

A bronze figure of a negro slave cleaning a boot.

slave. Slaves cost good money, so it was better to have them flogged.

If a slave killed his master, **all** the master's slaves had to be put to death. Even those who were innocent had to die. The law said that they should have stopped the murderer.

In law, slaves could not own money or anything else. But this rule was not always kept. Some slaves got tips from their masters. Some did business deals 'on the side'. Slaves who were skilled craftsmen could earn a great deal. So some slaves were able to save up enough to buy their freedom (see Section C).

Now try Exercise 9.2.

Exercise 9.2

Read **Section B** and **Source 9c**, then answer the questions. Each answer should consist of *two* sentences.

a Which character spoke the words in **Source 9c**? Was he a real slave?

b Who wrote **Source 9c**? Is it fact or fiction?

c Was the author of **Source 9c** a slave? Did he own slaves?

d Were Romans allowed to flog their slaves? Did they ever give them presents?

e Do you think that **Source 9c** gives a good idea of how slaves thought?

A draper's shop. The draper's slaves hold up the material for the customers to inspect.

C Into and out of slavery

Rome's army brought in a lot of slaves. The soldiers killed some of their prisoners, but those they spared became slaves. After a war in Greece in 167 BC, the general sent 50,000 prisoners to Rome to be sold. The general got the money.

For some, slavery was a punishment for a crime. The courts could condemn men or women to be sold if they were found guilty of a serious crime. There was no escape. Those sentenced to slavery were slaves for life.

In Rome it was true that some men and women were born slaves. The children of slaves were slaves themselves. The law said that if your mother was a slave, **you** were a slave.

No-one liked being a slave. Some ran away, but if they were caught they could be killed. From time to time, there was a slave revolt. In 73 BC, **Spartacus** led huge armies of runaway slaves in Sicily and southern Italy. The revolt was crushed, and thousands of slaves were crucified along the road to Rome.

Slaves could **buy** their freedom, or they could be **given** it. Slaves who managed to earn or save some money could **pay** their masters to set them free. Some kind masters **gave** faithful slaves their freedom as a reward for years of service. Some rich Romans, when they died, left wills saying that their most trusted slaves had to be set free.

Someone who had been a slave and was now free was called a **freedman** or **freedwoman**. Some freedmen became merchants, grew rich, and bought slaves themselves. Freedman were kept out of some jobs, but their children were completely free. At least one Roman emperor was the son of a freedman, that is, the son of a former slave.

Now try Exercise 9.3.

A freedwoman's tombstone in South Shields. She was the slave of a merchant called Barates. He set her free and married her.

Exercise 9.3

Read **Section C**, and look at **Source 9b**.

a How did men and women become slaves? (Find three ways of becoming a slave.)
b How did some slaves get their freedom? (Find three ways of getting free.)
c What did Roman masters do to stop their slaves escaping? (Write down two things they did, then draw **Source 9a** or **Source 9b**.)

Source 9e

Your bailiff should be able to read and write, and know everything about farming. Don't let him use a whip if he can get the same results without one. Slaves work better if you treat them well. Give them extra food or clothing and days off work. Let them take wives among the female slaves. This will make them more loyal to the farm, and to you.

Written by a Roman called Varro in about 40 BC.

Fact and Opinion

A **fact** is something which is or was true. It is a **fact** that the Romans invaded Britain in AD 43.

An **opinion** is what someone thinks or thought. It was Hadrian's **opinion** that if the Romans built a wall across Britain they would find it easier to keep the northern tribes in order.

Source 9d

Does Rutilus believe that slaves are the same as their masters? Not on your life. Nothing pleases him more than a good flogging. He loves the crack of the lash. He's a monster to his household. He's never so happy as when some poor slave who has stolen a couple of towels is being branded with red-hot irons. His chief pleasures are dungeons, burnt flesh, and field labour camps.

Written by the Roman poet Juvenal in about AD 110.

Exercise 9.4

Read **Sources 9d** and **9e** and the note on 'Fact and Opinion'.

a **Facts** – how were slaves punished? Write down four different punishments mentioned in **Source 9d.**
b What was Rutilus's **opinion** (**Source 9d**) on how to treat slaves?
c Does Juvenal (the author of **Source 9d**) say what he thought about how you should treat slaves? What do you think his **opinion** was? (Write two sentences.)
d What was Varro's **opinion** (Source 9e) about the right sort of man to have as a farm foreman? (Write a sentence).
e What were Varro's **opinions** on how you should treat slaves? (Write two or three sentences).

Exercise 9.5

Students of history do not all have the same **opinions** about the past. For example, some think that the Romans were cruel, and treated their slaves worse than animals. On the other hand, some students think that Romans were quite kind to their slaves.

Do *you* think that the Romans treated their slaves well or badly? Discuss this question in a group. Think about the facts in this chapter, and **Sources 9d** and **9e**.

Either **a**) Make a chart or wall-display or **b**) Make a group tape.

Education and the Law

Source 10a

I can do without you, you awful school-teacher. You do nothing but bring misery to poor boys and girls. I am wakened by the noise of your voice and the lash of your strap before the first cock crows in the morning. I wish you would send your pupils home. Would you take as much money to keep quiet as you earn from the noise you make?

From a Latin poem by Martial, who lived from AD 40 to AD 104.

Source 10b

A wooden writing tablet and a metal stylus.

An abacus.

A Schools

The law did not force Roman children to go to school. But in Rome and other towns and cities, most parents sent their children to a **master**. He taught them to read and write and do arithmetic. The parents paid him fees. (That was the only money the master got.)

A Roman school was small. It might be a shed, or a room in the master's house. It could be a part of the street, with only a curtain between the pupils and the passers-by. There were no desks, just some benches and chairs. The pupils wrote with a **stylus** (see Source 10b) on a wooden tablet, which was covered in wax. They did sums on an abacus.

Source 10c

No school-teacher gets a proper wage. You start before it's light in the morning. You have to work in a little room that no blacksmith would put up with. Your pupils bring dirty lanterns and make the books black from front to back. The parents are never satisfied, and you have to force them to pay their fees. And in a whole year you earn as much as a jockey gets for one race.

From a Latin poem by Juvenal, who lived from AD 55 to AD 140.

A first century AD inkpot and pen.

Girls as well as boys went to these one-teacher schools. The masters shouted at boys and girls alike, and beat them when they were slow, or lazy, or badly behaved.

Daughters of rich Romans stayed at home. They were taught by a **tutor**, probably a Greek slave. Well-off parents had another slave to take their sons to school. If a boy misbehaved, it was the slave's job to flog him. If he did not do it hard enough, the boy's father flogged the slave.

Poor Romans learned to read and write, and not much more. But boys from rich homes went on to **grammar** masters. 'Grammar' meant the Greek language, as well as Latin. It also meant the books of the great Greek and Roman authors, such as Homer and Virgil.

The last stage in the schooling of a well-off Roman was to learn **rhetoric** and the law. Rhetoric means speaking well in public. It was important, for Romans judged men on how well they spoke. In the early days of Rome, all the top jobs went to the best public speakers.

Now try Exercises 10.1, 10.2 and 10.3.

Source 10d

A teacher with his pupils. Archaeologists call this carving, 'arriving late for school'. Greeks often wore beards. Most Romans were clean-shaven. Roman books were written on rolls of papyrus, a kind of a paper made from a plant that grew in Egypt. You had to unroll the book as you read it.

Exercise 10.1

Read **Section A** and **Sources 10a** and **10c**. Study **Sources 10b** and **10d**.

a Write down four **facts** about schools that we can learn from **Sources 10a** and **10c**.
b Write down three **facts** about teachers, books, and writing that we can learn from **Sources 10b** and **10d**.
c Draw a picture of a Roman book.

Exercise 10.2

Read **Sources 10a** and **10c** again, then answer the questions.

a Who wrote **Source 10a**, and when did he live? (Write a sentence.)

b Who wrote **Source 10c**, and when did he live? (Write a sentence.)

c What was Martial's opinion of teachers? Did he like them? (Write two or three sentences.)

d What was Juvenal's opinion of teachers? Was he on their side? (Write two or three sentences.)

Exercise 10.3

How could we try to find out more about Roman schools

a How would each of the following help? (Write at least one sentence about each.)
  i Reading books, poems, or plays by Roman authors.
  ii Looking at Roman statues, carvings, and pictures (e.g. mosaics).
  iii Looking at things in museums (e.g. a stylus, an abacus, a writing tablet).

b Why would it be useless to try to do the following things? (Write at least one sentence about each.)
  iv Talking to old people who had been taught in Roman schools.
  v Looking at photographs or films of Roman schools at work.

(If you wish, you could discuss the above questions in a group. Then, either one person in the group could make a short speech to the rest of the class, saying what you all think; or each person in the group could write down what he or she thinks are the best ideas).

The bronze statue of an orator.

B Orators

All high-class Romans studied the law. Young men made their names by speaking in the courts. They became well known as **orators** (or speakers). Crowds packed the benches in the courts to listen to their speeches, and admire their tricks.

Trials in the courts were contests between two sides. For example, Marcus would say that Brutus had stolen his money, and Brutus would say he had not. Marcus would hire an orator to speak for him. So Brutus would get one too.

A judge and jury heard the case. At the end, they decided who was right. They also fixed the punishment. Who won, and what the sentence was, depended partly on how good the orators had been.

Source 10e

I was the orator for a senator's daughter. Her father, who was 80 years old, had married again and cut his daughter out of his will. She was suing him for a fair share of his money.

The case was heard by a jury of 180 men (four times the normal size). Each side had its crowd of supporters filling the front seats. There were several rows of spectators as well. Men and women were hanging over the rails, keen to see and hear what was going on. I made a very good speech. Some of my friends think it was the best I have ever made. But in the end the jury was split, half for us, and half against.

From a letter written by Pliny in about AD 105.

A basilica or law court (in Pompeii). In Roman times the building had a roof. The judges sat on a platform at one end.

Marcus and Brutus took all their friends to court with them. The friends clapped and cheered at the end of their orator's speech. They hoped the jury would be impressed, and vote for their side. And it was common for an orator to hire **clappers** to fill the public benches, and clap when he gave the nod.

Now try Exercise 10.4.

Exercise 10.4

Read **Section B** and **Source 10e**, then answer the questions in sentences.

a How did young men become famous in Rome?
b Why did Marcus and Brutus hire orators?
c Why did men involved in cases take their friends to court?
d What did 'clappers' do?
e In **Source 10e**, Pliny says he was the orator for whom?
f In **Source 10e**, what was the case about?
g How big was a normal jury (see **Source 10e**)?
h Which sentence in **Source 10e** tells us that Romans were interested in court cases?

C Crime and punishment

Unlike most states at that time, Rome had written laws. The laws were first written down in about 450 BC. **The Twelve Tables**, as they were then called, said what was against the law, and what the punishments were. New laws were added after that, and they too were written down. So all Romans knew what the law allowed.

On the whole, Roman trials were fair. They were held in public, so people could see what was going on. **Witnesses** said what they knew against the accused, and the accused had the right to question them. He could also speak in his own defence. (Or his orator could do these things for him.) And Romans who were found guilty could appeal to the emperor.

The **sentence** depended on who the guilty person was. Rich men or women would be fined or sent into **exile** (made to leave Rome). In the worst cases, they were sentenced to death. But they got the chance to take their own lives, to save them from the shame of a public execution.

The poor could not be fined, for they had no money. Instead, they were condemned to slavery, and sent in chains to the fields or the mines. For a lot of crimes, though, the penalty was death. Poor Romans were burnt alive, or beheaded, or hanged. But for a lot of them, a sentence of death meant being torn apart by wild beasts in a public show.

Now try Exercise 10.5.

Exercise 10.5

Read **Section C**, and look back at Section B. Write sentences to show that you know the meaning of these words and phrases:

a Orators
b Jury
c 'The Twelve Tables'
d Witnesses
e The accused
f Appeal to the emperor
g Exile
h Execution

Right: a carving from the first century AD, showing a man being killed by a lion in the circus.

Below: various Roman punishments for both rich and poor criminals.

The Family

A Father's word is law

The Roman empire was run by men. All the senators were men, and so were the judges and juries. And the man was the boss in the home as well. The law said the father was the head of the household. 'Household' meant his wife, sons and daughters, grandchildren, and slaves.

The father was a judge in his home. His duty was to correct and punish those who did wrong. In early Rome, he had huge powers. He could throw his children out of the home, and sell them as slaves. He could even have them, or his slaves, put to death.

Until the fourth century AD, a father could order a new-born child to be **exposed** (left outdoors to die). Poor parents sometimes did this. Fathers who wanted sons would expose new-born daughters. But often a childless couple would find an exposed infant and bring it up as their own.

By the end of the fourth century, though, the power of the Roman father had been cut. He could no longer make slaves of his children. He could not put his sons and daughters, or even his slaves, to death. He was not allowed to expose infant children.

But men were still the heads of their families. Girls obeyed their fathers before they were married, and their husbands after. They had to be good wives and mothers, and manage the house. If husband and wife fell out,

divorce was easy — the man just sent his wife back to her father.

It would be wrong, though, to think that all Roman men were tyrants. Most of them did not use their great power. Romans enjoyed spending time with their families. There are lots of signs that they really loved their wives and children (daughters as well as sons).

Now try Exercise 11.1.

Change

History is about change, but things do not all change at the same rate. Some things do not change at all for long periods of time.

There was a big change in Rome between 100 BC and AD 1. In 100 BC it was a **republic**. But by AD 1 it had an **emperor**. On the other hand, the army did not change much. Soldiers fought with swords and spears in 100 BC. They used the same weapons in AD 1.

Left: Children fighting.

Far left: A portrait of a young married couple.

Exercise 11.1

Read **Section A** and the notes on 'Change'. How did the powers of a Roman father change as time passed? There are six questions and two columns in the chart below — for 'early Rome' and for 'Rome at the end of the fourth century AD'. In each blank space, write 'Yes' or 'No' as the answer to the question.

	Early Rome	End of fourth century
a Was the father head of the family?		
b Could the father have his children put to death?		
c Could the father have his slaves put to death?		
d Could the father sell his children as slaves?		
e Could the father have newborn children exposed?		
f Could the man divorce his wife?		

B Marriage

Marriage in Rome was a deal between families. The two fathers decided who should marry whom, and when. They also agreed on the size of the **dowry**. The dowry was the sum of money the girl's father paid to the bridegroom. Well-off Romans would not dream of letting their sons marry girls whose fathers could not afford a decent dowry.

Girls got married in their early teens. (Their husbands were a few years older.) At that age, girls married the men their fathers chose. But marriage was not always for life. A lot of Romans died young, and divorce was easy. Some men and women got married three or four times. When they were older, they could choose for themselves.

For her wedding, the bride wore a long white robe with a red or yellow veil. The guests met in the bride's father's house, and that is where the couple made their marriage vows. Then the couple and the guests walked in procession to the bridegroom's house. When they arrived, the groom carried his bride over the threshold. Finally, they all joined in a great feast.

Now try Exercises 11.2 and 11.3.

Source 11a

A marriage ceremony. This was carved in the second century AD, and was the lid of a sarcophagus (coffin).

Exercise 11.2

Read **Section B** and look at **Source 11a**. Write TRUE or FALSE after each of the sentences below.

a Roman girls did not marry before the age of eighteen. _____
b Bridegrooms were normally older than brides. _____
c Romans liked their sons to marry girls who had plenty of money.
   _____
d Roman girls chose their own husbands. _____
e A dowry was a payment made by a man to his wife's father.
   _____
f A Roman bride wore a coloured veil. _____
g The bride and bridegroom held hands as they made their vows.
   _____
h The bride and bridegroom knelt as they made their vows.
   _____

Source 11b

I think more rich men should marry poor men's daughters, girls with no dowries. It would save them money in the end. Their wives would not be able to say, 'You got a big dowry when you married me, so you should spend more money on me. I want more clothes and slaves and carriages'.

From a speech by a character called Megadorus in a play by the Roman author Plautus.

Source 11c

You ought to want to please your husband. I've given you food, clothes, jewels, everything you could need. But if you go on like this, I'll divorce you and send you back to your father. Every time I go out, you want to know where I'm going. When I come in, you want to know what I've brought back. I might as well be married to a policeman.

From a speech by Menaechmus in another play by Plautus.

Source 11d

My neighbour liked what he heard about my son. So he told me he wanted him to marry his daughter. And he offered a good dowry. We both agreed to the plan, and fixed today for the wedding.

From a speech by a character called Simo in a play by the Roman author Terence. He wrote the play in 166 BC.

Exercise 11.3

Read **Sources 11b**, **11c**, and **11d**. (Either do this exercise on your own or in a group. If you do it in a group, you may either write down your answers, or make a tape or cassette.)

a Write a paragraph about **Sources 11b, 11c,** and **11d.** Answer these questions:
  i Where do the sources come from?
  ii Who were the characters who made the speeches?
  iii Are the sources fact or fiction?
b What do the sources tell us about marriage in Rome? Write a paragraph answering these questions:
  i What do they say about arranged marriages and dowries?
  ii What do they say about how husbands and wives spoke to each other?
  iii What do they say about divorce?
c Should we trust what these sources tell us about marriage and family life? Or are they just stories to amuse people?

(Write a paragraph saying what you think.)

C Rich and poor women

Not many women in Rome went out to work. There were some women teachers, and a few women doctors. There were also female nurses, dressmakers, and hairdressers. But most women stayed at home.

A poor woman was always busy. She had to look after the children, cook the meals, and clean the house, with no slaves to help her. She had to carry water from the public fountain,

A young woman having her hair arranged by a slave.

A rich woman playing the kithara – from about 50 BC.

through the streets, and up the stairs. In her spare time, she mended the family's clothes, and made new ones. The only thing she did not do was the shopping — the men did that.

A rich woman had slaves to do the housework. Her job was to make sure that they were not lazy or careless. Her older daughters helped her. Neither she nor they went out to work. A well-off woman could spend time reading, or writing letters, or visiting friends. Sometimes she went to the theatre, or the chariot races, or a grand dinner party. Rich women had an easy life, and so did their husbands.

Now try Exercises 11.4 and 11.5.

Source 11e

When a woman is busy with her make-up, her face is lost under a damp bread face-pack. Or else it is covered in greasy cream. When they are wiped off, she puts on the Indian scents and lotions. Next, she freshens her complexion with asses' milk. If her husband gets a job in the far north, a herd of asses will go with them.

Written by the poet Juvenal in about AD 110.

Source 11f

If she's in a bad mood, the slaves are for it! One has rods broken over his back. Another gets stripes from the whip. A third gets lashed with the cat-o-nine-tails. While this is going on, she'll be fixing her face, gossiping with friends, or thinking about a new dress.

Written by the poet Juvenal in about AD 110.

Exercise 11.4

Read **Section C**, and make your own notes.

a Write down four jobs that poor women had to do.
b Write a sentence explaining why rich women had plenty of spare time.
c Write down four things that rich women were able to do in their spare time.

Exercise 11.5

Read **Sources 11e** and **11f**, then answer the questions.

a What does **Source 11e** tell us about make-up? (Write a sentence.)
b **Source 11f** tells us that some Roman women had the power to do what? (Write a sentence.)
c Are **Sources 11e** and **11f** about rich women or poor women? (Write two or three sentences. Give at least one reason for your answer.)
d Does the author tell us his **opinions** in either **Source 11e** or **Source 11f**, or does he just give us some facts? (Write a sentence.)
e What do you think are the author's opinions of the women and the slaves in **Sources 11e** and **11f**? (Write a paragraph, saying how the author shows us what he thinks.)
f Draw a cartoon of something described in **Source 11e** or **Source 11f**.

12 Roman Religion

A first century AD statue of Neptune, the god of the sea.

A The Roman gods

The Romans believed in a lot of gods and goddesses. (Look at the table on page 62.) **Jupiter** and **Juno** were the most important ones. Every army camp had a chapel with an altar to Jupiter. This was where the cohort's standard or the legion's 'eagle' was kept in time of peace.

The Romans tried to keep on good terms with all of the gods. If they were crossing the sea, they asked for **Neptune's** help. If they went hunting, they prayed to **Diana.**

As well as the main gods of Rome, there were the **'household gods'**. Romans believed that a god looked after the family and its head, and that spirits cared for the home. So they had a little shrine in each house. They kept

A wall painting of Venus, rising out of the sea. This was how she was born, according to the legend.

A shrine to the lares, the household gods.

a flame burning there, and prayed before it each day.

Romans also worshipped their past **emperors**. They said that emperors became gods when they died. The chiefs of conquered nations had to serve as priests in the emperors' temples. This was a way of making them show that they were loyal to Rome.

The Romans allowed the conquered peoples to pray to their own gods. But they had to worship Rome's gods **as well**. Altars and carvings that have been found tell us that the Britons kept their own gods. They also show that some Romans prayed to the British gods too. The Romans must have thought that it was as well to keep on the right side of them.

Now try Exercise 12.1.

The head of Cybele, goddess of forests and wild animals.

Roman gods and goddesses

Name	What job did he or she do?
Jupiter	King of the gods, protector of Rome, sky god
Juno	Queen of the gods, moon goddess, guardian of women
Minerva	Goddess of war, goddess of craftsmen
Mars	God of war
Neptune	God of the sea
Apollo	God of healing (his priests could foretell the future)
Vulcan	God of fire and volcanoes, god of blacksmiths
Ceres	Goddess of corn and harvests
Mercury	God of traders and merchants, messenger of the gods
Diana	Goddess of hunters and wild places
Venus	Goddess of love and flowers
Vesta	Goddess of the fireplace and the home
Saturn	God of farming, Jupiter's father
Bacchus	God of wine

Exercise 12.1

Read **Section A**, and look at the table. Fill in the blank spaces in the sentences.

a _____ was the queen of the Roman gods.

b _____ was the goddess of war, and _____ was the god of war.

c Minerva was also the goddess of _____

d Romans thought that _____'s priests could see into the future.

e Farmers hoped that _____ would be kind and send a good harvest.

f _____ was the special god of merchants.

g Housewives asked _____ to keep their fires alight.

h Saturn was _____'s father.

B Temples and festivals

Each god and goddess had his or her own temples. Even a small town would have six or seven temples. But there were no full-time priests — the job was done by the leading men in the town. (There were a few exceptions. One was the temple of the goddess Vesta in Rome. It was looked after by girls and young women called the 'Vestal Virgins'.)

The Romans thought that it was important to keep the gods happy. This meant they had to go to the temples and make sacrifices (such as an ox or a sheep) at the right times. If they did not bother, they believed that the gods would be angry, and punish them. The gods might send an earthquake, an outbreak of disease, or make the Romans lose a battle.

They made the sacrifices at the time of the festivals. There were a lot of these. Each god and goddess had at least one a year. The biggest was **Saturnalia** (the festival of Saturn) in December. This is when Romans gave each other presents and went to parties. It was also the time when they set the slaves free for a few days.

A festival was the only time when a crowd gathered at a temple. At other times, men and women went there alone. Often they came to ask the god for help (e.g. before a long journey). When they did that, they had to give the god a present. It might be money, or a piece of gold or silver, or a new stone altar.

Now try Exercise 12.2.

A wall painting from Pompeii showing a bull being led to sacrifice.

A model of the temple of Claudius at Colchester.

The temple of Vesta in Rome.

Exercise 12.2

a Read **Section B**. Then write sentences to show that you know what these words mean.

i   Temple   v   Festival
ii Priest   vi Saturnalia
iii Vestal Virgins vii Altar
iv Sacrifice

b Make a drawing of a Roman temple.

C Christianity

The **Christians** were the followers of **Jesus**. He was a Jew, whom the Romans put to death in about AD 30. Christians, like Jews, said there was only **one** God. They would not worship the gods of Rome. For this, the Romans threw some of them into prison, and put some to death.

The Christian religion spread fast. (It was popular with the poor and the slaves.) Soon, there were Christians in Rome. Emperor Nero blamed them for the great fire which destroyed a large part of Rome in AD 64. He condemned many Christians to death, and a lot of them died in his public shows.

The numbers of Christians went on growing. The laws against them were not always enforced. But when there was an outbreak of plague or a bad harvest, men said that the gods were angry. They blamed the Christians, and the killings began again.

Just after AD 300 the Romans changed their minds. The emperor Constantine said the Christians were free to worship in their own way. Later, he became a Christian himself. By the year AD 400, most Romans were Christians. The temples of the old gods were closed down.

Now try Exercise 12.3.

Emperor Constantine.

Exercise 12.3

Write out the events below in the correct order (earliest first). Write the dates, the events, and say which century each event happened in. (All the dates are AD.)

337 Emperor Constantine became a Christian.
432 St. Patrick began preaching Christianity in Ireland.
64 Nero blamed the Christians for the fire of Rome.
391 The worship of the old Roman gods was banned.
250 All men in the empire were ordered to pray to the Roman gods.
208 St. Alban was put to death by the Romans in Britain for being a Christian.
313 Emperor Constantine gave Christians the right to worship freely.

Draw a time line, showing the above events and naming the centuries.

Source 12a

The town of Delphi stands on Mount Parnassus in Greece. This is where the snake called Python once lived. (Python had been sent by the goddess Juno.) But the god Apollo killed the snake with an arrow. And Delphi is now a holy place of Apollo.

From a Latin poem by Lucan, who lived from AD 39 to AD 65.

Source 12b

The earth gave birth to a great snake. Its name was Python. It was so big that it covered the whole hillside at Delphi. At last, the god Apollo came to deal with it. But he needed a thousand arrows to kill it. To mark what he had done, Apollo started the Pythian games. Young men came from all parts of Greece to take part in the wrestling, running, and chariot-races.

From a Latin poem by Ovid, who lived from 43 BC to AD 17. Mount Parnassus and Delphi are real places. There was a temple of Apollo at Delphi. The Pythian Games were held there every four years.

Exercise 12.4

Read **Sources 12a** and **12b**.

a Write down three things that are in **Source 12a**, but not in **Source 12b**.
b Write down three things that are in **Source 12b**, but not in **Source 12a**.
c Write down three things that are in both sources.
d Is there any truth in Sources **12a** and **12b**? Write down any things that are true.
e Which parts of **Sources 12a** and **12b** do you think are fiction (made up)?

Source 12c

The Christians must not be hunted out. If they are named and proved to be Christians they must be punished. If someone says he is not a Christian, and proves it by praying to the Roman gods, then let him off. He has repented, and that will do.

A letter from Trajan, who was Roman emperor from AD 98 to AD 117.

Source 12d

Behave well so that even the pagans (Romans) will see that you are good people. They call you criminals now, but they will see that you live good lives. Obey the law and emperor. Obey the judge who condemns you as criminals. It is God's will that you should show up these stupid people for what they are.

Part of a letter from St. Peter to the Christians of Asia Minor.

Exercise 12.5

Read **Sources 12c** and **12d**.

a Who wrote **Source 12c**, and when did he write it? (Write a sentence.)
b Was the author of **Source 12c** a Christian? (Write at least one sentence, giving your reasons.)
c **Source 12c** says that a person could prove he was not a Christian by doing what? (Write a sentence.)
d Who wrote **Source 12d**? (Write a sentence).
e Mention two things that the author of **Source 12d** wanted the Christians to do. (Write two sentences.)
f Who do you think were 'these stupid people' in **Source 12d**? (Write a sentence.)
g Did the authors of **Sources 12c** and **12d** have different points of view? (Write a paragraph, explaining what you think.)

In some villas there are mosaics with Christian pictures. In the centre of this mosaic you can see a picture of Jesus.

13 Leisure and Entertainment

The hot room in the baths at Pompeii.

Source 13a

I live right over a public bath-house. You can imagine what noise I have to put up with. I can hear men gasping as they do their exercises. I hear the smacking of flesh as someone gets a massage. Then a ballplayer comes along, shouting out the score.

Some days, there's the noise of a fight, or someone caught stealing. There's the man who sings in the bath, and people who jump into the pool with a splash. On top of all this, I can hear the cries of the men selling drinks, sausages, and pastries.

Written by Seneca in about AD 60.

A The baths

Every afternoon, Romans went to the baths, but not just to wash. They went there to meet their friends, hear the news, play games, and perhaps have a snack to eat. The baths were part of Roman life. They were mainly for the men, but women were allowed to use them at special times. Mixed bathing was not allowed.

Rome had hundreds of bath-houses. Some were large and grand, with marble halls and pillars. Some were free, and none charged more than a few pence. Every town had at least one set of public baths. Each army fort had its bath-house. Most villas had their own baths.

In the bath-house, the Roman undressed, then went through three or four rooms, cold, then warm, then hot. (The heat came from under the floor.) In the hottest room, his slave poured olive oil onto his skin, then scraped him with a metal tool. (There was no soap.) Finally, he dived into the plunge bath to wash off the oil.

Now try Exercise 13.1.

Exercise 13.1

Read **Section A** and **Source 13a**. Write down *eight* different noises that Seneca complains about.

B **The theatre**

As you read in Chapter 12, the Roman year was full of festivals. On the first day of each festival, there were plays in the theatre. Rich Romans paid the actors, and entry was free for the common people.

The theatres, and a lot of the plays, were copied from the Greeks. The theatres were built of stone, with stone seats in tiers, and no roof. (Look at Source 13b.) Plays were performed in the daytime, so there was no need for lights. The city's leading men and their wives sat in the best seats, at the front.

But there was room for the poor as well. Even slaves were allowed in, to stand at the back.

The plays were either **tragedies** (serious plays) or **comedies**. In the early days of Rome, all the actors were men, and they wore masks to show which parts they were playing. But in later years in Rome, singing and dancing shows became more popular than plays. And for the first time, women as well as men appeared on the stage.

Now try Exercise 13.2.

A mosaic of a mask which was worn when a tragedy was performed.

Source **13b**

The theatre at Pompeii.

Exercise 13.2

Read **Section B** and look at **Source 13b**. Find at least *six* differences between:
a Roman theatres and the plays performed in the early days of Rome, and
b modern theatres and plays.

Source 13c

When the Colosseum was opened, emperor Titus put on a big show, with a lot of gladiators. There was also a sea-battle on a lake. When they let the water out, they used the basin for more fights and a wild-beast hunt. Five thousand beasts were killed in one day.

Written by Suetonius in AD 120. The Colosseum was opened in AD 80.

Source 13d

Wasting your time at a show makes you more cruel and less decent. I went to one of them at lunch-time, hoping for a change from all the killing. Far from it! In the morning, men were thrown to the lions and bears. But at lunch-time it was man against man. The fighters had nothing to protect them from the weapons – no helmets or shields. The crowd shouted, 'Kill him! Flog him! Burn him!'

Written by Seneca in about AD 60.

A fragment of Roman glass, showing a gladiator, AD 400.

C Gladiators and wild animals

Romans also loved to go to see the **gladiators**. These were slaves or condemned men, trained to fight, and ready to die. Normally a man armed with sword and shield took on one with a net and spear. Sometimes men fought lions, or tigers, or bears. Sometimes the wild beasts fought each other, or tore condemned criminals apart.

The shows took place in **amphitheatres**. These were large oval stadiums, built either of stone or earth. There was a central arena, where the fighting took place. Round it were the rows of banked seats. The Colosseum in Rome had room for 50,000 people. (Look at Source 13f.)

Rich Romans paid for the shows. Entry for the poor was free. The emperor himself often gave a show to please the common folk. When he attended, he sat in a special box. The gladiators saluted him before they fought. And if both men were alive at the end, he decided whether the loser was to live or die.

Now try Exercises 13.3, 13.4 and 13.5.

Source 13e

I put on three gladiator shows in my own name, and five in the names of my sons and grandsons. About 10,000 men fought in them. I put on 26 shows with wild animals from Africa. About 3,500 beasts were killed.

Written by the emperor Augustus in about AD 10.

Inside the Colosseum in Rome. The floor of the arena has been removed. You can see the cells and cages where the prisoners, gladiators and animals were kept.

Exercise 13.3

Read **Section C** and Sources **13c**, **13d**, and **13e**. Write your answers in sentences.

a What is a primary source?
b When was the Colosseum opened? When did Suetonius (**Source 13c**) write?
c Is it possible that **Source 13c** is a primary source? (Explain your answer.)
d Write out a sentence from **Source 13d** to show that it is a primary source.
e Write out a sentence from **Source 13e** to show that it is a primary source.

Exercise 13.4

Read **Sources 13c, 13d**, and **13e** again.

a Write down four facts from **Source 13c**.
b Write down three facts from **Source 13d**.
c What was Seneca's opinion of the show? (**Source 13d**)
d What was the crowd's opinion of the show? (**Source 13d**)
e Write down three facts from **Source 13e**.
f Does **Source 13e** contain any opinions?

Exercise 13.5

Read again the note on **Motives** on page 43. Discuss these questions in a group. Make your answers into a group tape, or write them out in sentences.

a **Source 13d** says that the crowd at the shows shouted what?
b What do you think were the **motives** of the people who went to watch the shows?
c Does emperor Augustus (**Source 13e**) say what his **motives** were for putting on the shows?
d What do you think were emperor Augustus's **motives**?
e Which *three* kinds of fighting took place when the Colosseum was opened? (see **Source 13c**.)
f What do you think were emperor Titus's **motives**? (**Source 13c**.)

Source 13g

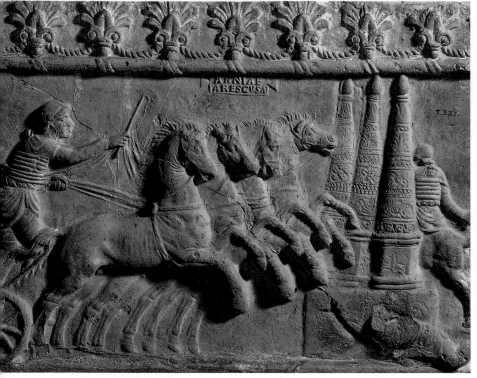

This carving from the first century AD shows a four horse chariot approaching the three columns of the turning post. A Jubilator, a rider who acts as a 'pacemaker', has already turned.

Source 13h

A model of the Circus Maximus in Rome.

D Chariot-racing

The favourite sport in Rome was chariot-racing. Everyone supported one of the racing teams — the Whites, the Reds, the Blues, or the Greens. On race days, huge crowds headed for the **Circus Maximus**, where the races took place.

Chariots were light, open, two-wheeled carts, drawn by two, three, or four horses. There were at least four of them in each race. They raced up a straight track, round a post at the end, and back again. A race was seven laps of the track. In a day's sport, there would be ten or twelve races.

There were lots of accidents. Quite often, horses and drivers were killed. But the best drivers became rich and famous. For them, the risks were worthwhile. The spectators took risks as well — there was heavy betting on the races.

Now try Exercise 13.6.

Exercise 13.6

Read **Section D**, and look at **Sources 13g** and **13h**.

a) Write notes (paragraph headings) for an essay answering these questions:
  i What can you find out about chariot racing by looking at **Sources 13g** and **13h**?
  ii What else could you find out if you visited the Circus Maximus in Rome (**Source 13h**)?
b Draw a picture of the Circus Maximus.

14 The End of the Roman Empire

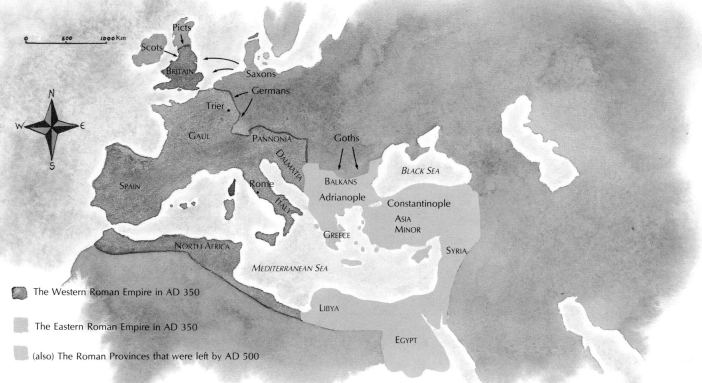

- The Western Roman Empire in AD 350
- The Eastern Roman Empire in AD 350
- (also) The Roman Provinces that were left by AD 500

A Rome's enemies

In the second century AD, Rome's empire stopped growing. In the third and fourth, it was under attack. Tribes of barbarians (**Germans** and **Goths**) invaded Gaul and the Balkans. (Look at the map.) They seized corn, cattle, gold, and silver. They also took people, and sold them as slaves.

Roman Britain suffered too. **Saxon** pirates from Germany crossed the sea to Britain. **Picts** attacked from the north. **Scots** (from Ireland) raided the west. To deal with the Saxons, the Romans built forts along the east and south coasts of England.

The Roman army's job was to defend the empire. It often failed to do so, partly because it was short of men. So the Romans let barbarians join their army, to keep the numbers up. Then they paid bribes to the tribes to keep

them at peace. In the end, they let the Goths settle in the Balkans. They hoped that this would put them on Rome's side.

Civil wars made things worse for Rome. Greedy generals tried to turn themselves into emperors. They marched their legions against each other, and not against the enemy. So the barbarians invaded while the Romans were away.

Between AD 284 and AD 337, though, there was a change for the better. Emperors **Diocletian** and **Constantine** made the army bigger and better. They built new forts and walls. They split the empire into two parts, east and west, to make it easier to rule. For a time, there was peace.

Now try Exercise 14.1.

This coin bears a picture of a Briton who was a soldier in the Roman Army. He got his men to call him 'Emperor Constantine III' and started a civil war.

The Roman Gate at Trier in eastern Gaul. The Romans built high walls round their towns and cities in the third and fourth centuries.

Exercise 14.1

Read **Section A**. Write TRUE or FALSE after each of the sentences below.

a The Roman empire did not get bigger after AD 200. _____

b The Germans and the Goths were barbarian nations. _____

c Britain was not attacked by barbarians. _____

d The Scots came from Ireland.
_____

e Barbarians were not allowed to join the Roman army.
_____

f The Goths paid bribes to the Romans. _____

g The barbarians did not know that the Romans were fighting civil wars. _____

h Diocletian and Constantine were strong emperors. _____

i Diocletian and Constantine stopped the barbarian attacks for a time. _____

B The fall of Rome

The good times did not last. The Goths in the Balkans fell out with the Romans. In AD 378, they beat a Roman army at **Adrianople**. They marched west, and threatened Rome itself.

This threat made the Romans remove their troops from Britain in AD 407. When the Saxons invaded again, the leading men in Britain begged the Romans to help. But the emperor said 'No'. He told the Britons that they would have to defend themselves.

In AD 410 the Goths sacked Rome. They killed, burned, and destroyed. They stole everything they could carry away. It is said that **Alaric**, their leader, took 500 pounds of gold and 30,000 pounds of silver from Rome. But the Goths were farmers, not city people.

They did not stay in Rome, and soon moved off to settle in Gaul and Spain.

The Roman empire was now in two parts, and had two emperors. One ruled the eastern part from Constantinople, and the other ruled the west from Rome. And the western part was falling apart. Barbarians conquered Gaul and Spain. They even reached north Africa.

Rome was sacked again in AD 455. The western empire was destroyed. The last emperor of the west was thrown out of Rome in AD 476. The eastern half of the empire did much better. It lasted for another thousand years.

Now try Exercise 14.2

Exercise 14.2

Read **Section B**, and study the Map on page 71.

a Which parts of the Roman empire did these provinces belong to in AD 350. (Write EAST or WEST in the spaces.)

  i Britain _____   **iii** Egypt _____   **v** Spain _____

  ii Gaul _____   **iv** Syria _____   **vi** Asia Minor _____

b Which provinces were still Roman in AD 500, and which had been lost? (Write ROMAN or LOST in the spaces.)

  i Greece _____   **iii** Spain _____   **v** Britain _____

  ii Balkans _____   **iv** Libya _____   **vi** Gaul _____

The head on this coin is that of Honorius, the emperor who told the Britons that they would have to defend themselves.

C Reasons for the fall of the Roman Empire

Why did the Roman empire come to an end? What were the **causes** of this great event? Hundreds of writers have tried to answer this question. They agree about some things, but not all. Sources 14a and 14b give you an idea of what two historians have said. Read both sources and try Exercise 14.3.

Source

Edward Gibbon's answer. (Not Gibbon's own words.)

1 Only free men are ready to fight for their country. The Romans stopped being free when they let the emperors take over. In the end, they were no more than slaves.
2 The Romans grew soft and lazy. The rich thought only about money. The poor cared for nothing but free bread and the chariot races.
3 There were civil wars all the time. The emperors could trust no-one.
4 The barbarians grew stronger.
5 The Romans let the barbarians live inside the empire.
6 The Romans let barbarians join the Roman army. In the end 'Roman' soldiers were just the same as their enemies.
7 After they became Christians, Romans did not want to fight. And the money which should have gone on soldiers' pay was spent on churches and priests.

From Gibbon's *The Decline and Fall of the Roman Empire.* He wrote this book between 1772 and 1788.

Source

Professor Chester Starr's answer. (Not Professor Starr's own words.)

1 The Roman Empire was too large. It took weeks for orders to reach the armies.
2 The barbarians grew stronger. The Roman army was not able to keep them all out.
3 The Romans wasted money trying to bribe the barbarians.
4 The Romans let some barbarians come and live on Roman land.
5 A lot of barbarians joined the Roman army. They were no better armed or trained than Rome's enemies.
6 Wars and invasions meant that it was not safe to trade and travel. So there was less to buy in the markets. All the prices rose.
7 There were too many civil wars. Army leaders fought each other, not Rome's enemies.

From a book which Professor Starr wrote in 1982. Professor Starr is a teacher at an American University.

Exercise 14.3

The authors of **Sources 14a** and **14b** have both tried to answer the question 'Why did the Roman empire in the west come to an end?'. They agree about some things, and disagree about others.

Which things do they agree about? What do they disagree about? Read the list below of 'reasons' for the fall of the Roman empire.

1　The Roman empire was too large.
2　Under the emperors, the Romans were not free.
3　The Romans grew soft and lazy.
4　The barbarians grew stronger.
5　The Romans wasted money trying to bribe the barbarians.
6　The Romans let the barbarians live inside the empire.
7　The Romans let the barbarians join the Roman army.
8　There were too many civil wars.
9　It became unsafe to trade and travel.
10　Turning Christian weakened Rome.

a　Write down the *four* reasons from the above list that are mentioned in **both Source 14a** and **Source 14b**.
b　Write down the *three* reasons that are mentioned **only** in **Source 14a**.
c　Write down the *three* reasons that are mentioned **only** in **Source 14b**.

Evidence from archaeology

Some of the forts on Hadrian's Wall were repaired shortly after AD 367. Coins and pottery made between AD 380 and 410 have been found at places on Hadrian's Wall and just to the south. No coins or pottery made after AD 367 have been found in the forts to the north of Hadrian's Wall.

Source 14c

(In AD 367) the barbarians all attacked at once. Roman Britain was on its knees. The emperor sent Theodosius to Britain. He found bands of (Picts and Saxons), loaded with loot. He quickly drove them off. He rebuilt the cities. He put sentries back on Hadrian's Wall and repaired the forts. He dismissed the scouts who had been on duty (north of the wall). They had been taking bribes from the Picts, and telling them about our troops.

Written by a Roman called Ammianus in the fifth century AD.

Exercise 14.4

Read **Source 14c** and the notes on 'Evidence from archaeology'. Answer the questions in sentences.

a　Which source tells us who attacked Roman Britain and when?
b　What do **Source 14c** and 'Evidence from archaeology' tell us about the forts on Hadrian's Wall?
c　What does **Source 14c** say that Theodosius did with the scouts north of the wall?
d　What does archaeology tell us about the forts north of the wall **after** AD 367? Do you think that there were any soldiers there at that time?
e　**Source 14c** says something about the scouts north of the wall that archaeology does not tell us. What is that?
f　Which point in 'Evidence from archaeology' tells us that there were still Roman soldiers on Hadrian's Wall in AD 400?

The church of Santa Sophia (now a mosque), was built by Justinian in AD 532–537. The old eastern empire capital of Constantinople is now the Turkish city of Istanbul.

15 What we owe to Rome

A Technology

The Germans and Goths who conquered the western Roman empire were not used to living in towns. Their homes were wooden huts with thatched roofs. They travelled on forest tracks, not paved roads.

The Saxons were afraid of the Roman remains they found in Britain. They kept away from the towns. They burned down the villas. And they did not believe that mere men could have made the roads. They said that the Roman roads were the work of devils.

In most of Gaul, Spain, and Italy the new rulers admired the Romans, and tried to copy them. They learned to build in stone. They put mosaic pictures in their churches. Some of them even used the baths.

There was no **progress** in technology, though. It was more than 500 years before men began to build the great stone cathedrals. And when they did begin, they built like Romans. Their doorways and windows were round arches. Their roofs were held up

Source 15a

Arches in Rome. The basilica of Constantine built in AD 300.

Source 15b

Arches in Norwich Cathedral (built by the Normans in the twelfth century).

Source 15c

The Pantheon in Rome (built in the second century AD).

on Roman vaults. Later still, a **thousand** years after the sack of Rome, masons re-learned to make the dome.

Right through the Middle Ages, men used the Roman roads. Until about 200 years ago, no-one tried to build new ones. And when they did, the road-builders used the same methods as the Romans. They dug ditches at the roadside, so that the roads would not be swamped. They laid solid foundations. They built in layers of stone and gravel. And they gave their roads a curved surface, so that water would run off.

Technology today has caught up with and passed the Romans. But it took a long time to do so. In 1850, not many towns had water supplies as good as those of ancient Rome. Much later still, hardly any homes had central heating.

Now try exercise 15.1.

Exercise 15.1

Read **Section A** and look at **Sources 15a, 15b, 15c** and **15d**. Read again **Sections A** and **B** in Chapter 8 on pages 41–3.

a Look at **Sources 15a, 15b, 15c,** and **15d**. List *three* things which builders in the Middle Ages and modern times have copied from the Romans.

b List *four* ways in which the road-makers of 200 years ago copied from the Romans.

Source 15d

St Paul's Cathedral in London (built in the seventeenth century AD).

B Language

The Romans spoke Latin. Most of the people in the western part of the empire spoke a kind of Latin. But the Latin they spoke in Gaul was not the same as the Latin they spoke in Spain. Each province had its own kind of Latin.

In time, the Latin of Gaul turned into French. The Latin of Spain and Italy became Spanish and Italian. But a lot of words in these languages were, and still are, close to Latin. We say they have Latin **roots**.

The Romans did not conquer Germany. So the Germans and Goths did not speak Latin. Their language did not have Latin roots. But when they conquered the Roman lands, they learned the language of their new homes. Before long, the German rulers of Gaul were speaking French. But the invaders of Roman Britain, the Angles and Saxons, kept their German speech. (We call it 'old English'.) The Angles and Saxons drove the Britons west, to Wales, and learned nothing from them.

In 1066, the **Normans** (from France) conquered England. They spoke French, and they brought the French language to England. By the year 1400, the people of England were speaking a language that was a mixture of 'old English' and French. Out of this grew our modern English, which contains a lot of Latin words. These words come from the French of the Normans. And French comes from the Latin of the Romans.

Now try Exercises 15.2 and 15.3.

The letters carved in this inscription from Hadrian's Wall are exactly the same letters as we use today.

THE MAIN LANGUAGES IN WESTERN EUROPE TODAY

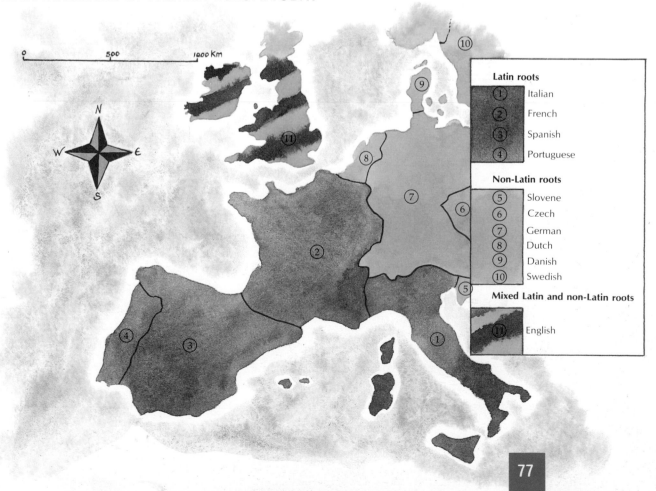

Latin roots
1. Italian
2. French
3. Spanish
4. Portuguese

Non-Latin roots
5. Slovene
6. Czech
7. German
8. Dutch
9. Danish
10. Swedish

Mixed Latin and non-Latin roots
11. English

Exercise 15.2

Read **Section B** and look at the Maps on pages 71 and 77. Answer the questions.

a Which of these modern languages have Latin roots: Dutch, Spanish, German, French, Italian, Danish?
b Why do some languages have Latin roots?
c Which two languages are now spoken in the Roman province of Spain?
d Which language is now spoken in most of the Roman province of Gaul?
e Which language is now spoken in most of the Roman province of Italy?
f Which language has a mixture of Latin and non-Latin roots?

Exercise 15.3

Study the 'Language Table' then answer the questions below.

a Which English words in the table are **similar** to Latin words?

_____

b Which English words in the table are **similar** to German words?

_____

c Write down the Latin and French words for
  i   Bread _____
  ii Hand _____
  iii Quarter _____

d Which three words are **exactly** the same in Latin and Italian? Write down the three words and their English meaning.

_____

e Write down the Latin and Spanish words for
  i   Arms _____
  ii End _____
  iii Moon _____

f How is the Spanish word for 'quarter' different from the Italian word for 'quarter'?

_____

A language table

English	Latin	French	Italian	Spanish	German
arms (weapons)	arma	armes	arma	armas	Waffen
bread	panis	pain	pane	pan	Brot
desert	deserta	desert	deserto	desierto	Wüste
end	finis	fin	fine	fin	Ende
hand	manus	main	mano	mano	Hand
moon	luna	lune	luna	luna	Mond
quarter	quarta	quart	quarto	cuarto	Viertel
sea	mare	mer	mare	mar	See

C Religion

Before the year AD 400, the Romans gave up their old gods. They turned from Jupiter and Juno to Jesus. Even when Rome fell, most parts of the empire remained Christian. At first, England did not. But in time, the Angles and Saxons, and the other peoples of Europe, were converted.

For a long time, the head of the whole church was the **Pope**, or Bishop of Rome. Christians said that St Peter, a disciple of Jesus, was the first Pope. (He was put to death by the emperor Nero in AD 64.)

Rome was the centre of the church. Latin was its language. The church service (the **Mass**) was in Latin, and so was the Bible. Only priests and monks could read and write. And they wrote their books and letters in Latin, of course.

The church did not stay united. In

AD 1054 the eastern church split from the west, and refused to obey the Pope. In the sixteenth century, the **Protestants** in the west did the same. But to **Roman Catholics**, the Pope is still the church's head. He is a link with St Peter and ancient Rome.

Not all Christians are Catholics today. And Catholics no longer use Latin for the Mass. Very few books are written in Latin today. But it was Rome that taught the western world to be Christian. And for many hundreds of years, Christians worshipped in the language of Rome.

Now try Exercise 15.4.

Exercise 15.4

Read **Section C**. Now fill in the missing words in each sentence, and decide whether it describes a change, or not. Write CHANGE or NO CHANGE in the brackets. Discuss the sentences in a group before you begin to write.

a Romans stopped worshipping their old gods and became _____ (_____)

b After the fall of the western empire, most provinces _____ Christian. (_____)

c For nearly a thousand years, the _____ was the head of the whole church. (_____)

d Between the years 1500 and 1600, the _____ stopped obeying the Pope. (_____)

e The Pope is still the head of the church for Roman _____ (_____)

f Today, Catholics no longer use _____ for the Mass. (_____)

This statue of Neptune was made in the seventeenth century AD, but was inspired by Roman statues like the one on page 61.

This famous painting of Venus by Sandro Botticelli (painted about 1480) was also inspired by the legend shown in the Roman picture on page 61.

Key Elements and corresponding exercises (those printed in bold type are particularly relevant)

Chapters	1	2	3	4	5	6	7	8	9	10	11	12	13	14	15

Key Element 1: Chronological knowledge and understanding

		1	2	3	4	5	6	7	8	9	10	11	12	13	14	15
a	Historical knowledge	1.2 1.4	2.1 2.5	3.1 3.3	4.3 4.4	5.2	6.3 6.4	7.1 7.2	8.2 8.3	9.1 9.3	10.1 10.2	11.2 11.3	12.1	13.2 13.6	14.1 14.2	15.2 15.4
b	Concepts and terminology	1.5	2.2		4.2	5.1	6.1				10.3		12.2			
c	Chronology – dates and sequence	1.1							8.4				12.3			
d	Chronology – conventions	**1.1**			**4.1**		6.3						12.3			15.4

Key Element 2: Range and depth of historical knowledge and understanding

		1	2	3	4	5	6	7	8	9	10	11	12	13	14	15
a	Cause and consequence					**5.4**	**6.4**			9.3						15.4
b	Motivation								**8.2**					13.5		
c	Continuity and change											**11.1**			14.2	15.4
d	Different features of situations				4.5			**7.4**			10.4		12.5			

Key Element 3: Awareness and understanding of interpretations of history

		1	2	3	4	5	6	7	8	9	10	11	12	13	14	15
a	Distinuishng fact and fiction	1.4						7.3		9.2		11.4	12.4			
b	Different versions of events and topics	1.4				5.2					10.4		12.4		14.4	
c	Recognizing fact and opinion									**9.4**		11.5		13.4		
d	Different interpretations		2.6	**3.5**	4.5					9.5						
e	Reasons for different interpretations			3.5		5.3				9.5						

Key Element 4: Knowledge and understanding of the processes of historical enquiry

		1	2	3	4	5	6	7	8	9	10	11	12	13	14	15
a	Acquiring information	1.3	2.1	3.1	4.4	5.5	6.2	7.2	8.3	9.1	10.2	11.3	12.1	13.1	14.1	15.3
b	Sources – authorship and dates		2.3	3.4				7.3			10.4		12.5		14.3	
c	Primary and secondary sources		**2.3**	3.4	4.3		6.2							13.3		
d	Making deductions from sources			**3.2**	4.3	5.5	6.2	**7.5**	8.1				12.5	13.6	14.4	
e	Using different kinds of source		2.4		4.2			7.5			10.1	11.2		13.2	14.4	15.1
f	Value and reliability of evidence					5.3	6.5			9.2	10.5	11.4				

Most of the exercises seek to develop organisational and communication skills (**Key Element 5**).